MEMOIRS

OF

DENZIL Lord HOLLES.

R.White sculp.

The Right Hon.ble
Denzel Baron Holles of Ifield.
Ætat. 78. año.1676. Ob:1679.

MEMOIRS

OF *Palk: Macki*

DENZIL
Lord HOLLES,

Baron of *Ifield* in *Suſſex*,

From the Year 1641, to 1648.

LONDON,

Printed for *Tim. Goodwin* at the Queen's
Head againſt St. *Dunſtan's* Church in *Fleet-
ſtreet.* M. DC. XC. IX.

(v)

To His Grace

J O H N

Duke of *Newcastle*, &c.

May it please your Grace;

WHEN the follow-
ing Papers of the
famous Lord *Hol-*
les, Your Great Uncle, happen'd to fall into my Hands,

A 3   I

I could not long deliberat
whether they deferv'd a public View, and therefore intended to get them printed
without any further Ceremo-
ny; for the large fhare he had
in the Tranfactions of thofe
Times will as much engage
others to read thefe Memoirs,
as the Defence he was oblig'd
to make for himfelf are a fufficient Reafon for his writing
them. But when I under-
ftood that Your Grace (out
of the Love You bear to vir-
tuous Actions, and Your Piety towards fo near a Relation) did order a ftately Monument to be erected at *Dor-
chefter* for this Illuftrious Perfon,

fon, I was of opinion, that as well for that Reafon, as be-caufe in his Life-time he en-tertain'd an extraordinary Af-fection and Efteem for You, Your Name fhould in like manner be infcrib'd on this Monument which he has left of Himfelf to Pofterity. The Juftice of the thing, and the Sincerity of my Intentions, muft be all my Apology to Your Grace for this Prefum-tion: for the Public (of whom You deferv'd fo well, and particularly in appearing early, like Your Noble An-ceftors, for the Liberty of thefe Nations) will acknow-ledg it an Obligation ; nor,

A 4   if

if any thing fhould chance to be amifs, can I doubt but an eafy Pardon will be granted to one who is, tho unknown, my Lord, with fo profound a Refpect, Your Grace's moft humble Servant.

March 28, 1699.

THE

THE
PUBLISHER
TO THE
READER.

SUch as really desire to know the naked Truth, and propose for their chiefest aim the common good (which are certainly the best, tho not the greatest part of Mankind) have ever exprest a desire in their Writings of seeing the Memoirs of all parties made public, as the most effectual means of framing a true General History : For in those places where nothing is licens'd to appear but what visibly tends to the advantage of one side, there can be no sincere representation of Affairs, the basest Cowards must pass for the bravest Heroes, the worst of Villains for the greatest Saints, the most

Ig-

Ignorant and Vicious for Men of Learning and Virtue, and the Enemies of their Country for its Preservers and Friends. Without consulting therefore the particular interest or reputation of any Faction, but only the benefit of England *in general, these Memoirs of the Great Lord* Holles *are communicated to the World, that by comparing them with those of* Ludlow, *and such as appear'd before, or will be publish'd hereafter relating to the same times, they may afford mutual Light to each other; and, after distinguishing the personal resentments or privat biasses of every one of 'em, the Truth wherein they are all found to agree (tho drest by them in different Garbs) may by som impartial and skilful hand be related with more candor, clearness, and uniformity. What figure our Author made in the Parliament and in the Wars, at home and abroad, in his privat and public Capacities, is generally known, and needs not therefore be mention'd in this place. The account he gives of himself in the fol-*

lowing

lowing *Papers* is confirm'd by many living *Witnesses,* as well as in the greatest part by other *Writers* of the same *Transactions.* But whether the vehemence of his *Stile,* the barbarous *Usage* he receiv'd, his concern for the *Presbyterian Party,* and his *Displeasure* at the *King's* misfortunes (to whom he was then an adherent and a friend) have not guided his *Pencil* to draw the lines of *Cromwel's* Face too strong, and the shadows too many, I refer to the judgment of the disinterested *Reader,* desiring him to allow all that is reasonably due to one in these or the like *Circumstances.* This caution *Justice* has oblig'd me to insert: For as to that tyrannical *Usurper* of the *Supreme Administration,* who prov'd so ungrateful to the *Commonwealth,* so treacherous to the *King,* and so fatal to both, I think him bad enough painted in his own true *Colours,* without standing in need of exaggerating *Rhetoric* to make him look more odious or deform'd. I should write something here likewise with relation to General Fairfax, but that the properest place, for it seems to be in a Preface to his own MEMORIAL, which is in good hands, and, it's hop'd, may be shortly expos'd to public view. How far soever King Charles the First's Enemies in England may look on themselves disoblig'd, or any of his Friends neglected by my Lord Holles, the Scots are surely beholding to him; for in his long Panegyric on that Nation, he has said more in their behalf than their own Historians have ever been able to offer. But in this and other matters of the like nature we shall not anticipate the Readers Curiosity or Judgment: I shall therefore only acquaint him, that tho this Piece be entitul'd Memorials from the History it contains, yet in substance it is an Apology for that Party who took up Arms, not to destroy the King, or alter the Constitution, but to restore the last, and oblige the former to rule according to Law.

To.

To the Unparallel'd Couple,
Mr. *Oliver* St. *John* his
Majefty's Sollicitor Gene-
ral, and Mr. *Oliver Cromwel*
the Parliament's Lieutenant
General, the two grand De-
figners of the Ruin of three
Kingdoms.

GENTLEMEN,

AS You have been principal
in miniftring the matter
of this Difcourfe, and giving me the leifure of making it,
by banifhing me from my Country and Bufinefs, fo is it reafon
I fhould particularly addrefs it to
You. You will find in it fome
reprefentation of the groffer Lines
of your Features, thofe outward
and notorious Enormities that make
You

You remarkable, and Your Pictures easie to be known; which cannot be expected here so fully to the Life as I could wish. He only can do that, whose Eye and Hand have been with You in Your secret Counsels, who has seen You at Your Meetings, Your Sabbaths, where You have laid by Your assumed Shapes (with which You cozen'd the World) and resumed Your own; imparting each to other, and both of You to Your fellow Witches, the bottom of Your Designs, the policy of Your Actings, the turns of Your Contrivances, all Your Falshoods, Cozenings, Villanies, and Cruelties, with Your full intentions to ruin the three Kingdoms. All I will say to You, is no more than what St. *Peter* said to *Simon* the Sorcerer, *Repent therefore of this Your wickedness, and pray God, if perhaps the thoughts of*
Your

Your Hearts may be forgiven You. And if You have not Grace to pray for Your ſelves (as it may be You have not) I have the Charity to do it for You, but not Faith e-nough to truſt You. So I remain, I thank God, not in Your Power, and as little at Your Service.

Denzil Holles.

At St. Mere Eglide in Nor-mandy, *this* 14th *of* Fe-bruary, 1648. S. V.

MEMOIRS

ERRATA.

PAge 15. line 22. read *Cromwel*, P. 39. l. 22. r. *written*. P. 43. l. 27. r. *publick*, P. 89. l. 7. dele *Comma*. L. 4. r. *Many in.* P. 96. l. 15. f. *the* r. *their.* P. 100. L. 18. r. *as to say.* P. 161. l. 8. dele *not*.

MEMOIRS

OF

Denzil Lord Hollis.

1. THE wiseft of Men faw it to be a great Evil, that Servants fhould ride on Horfes, and Princes walk as Servants on the Earth: An Evil now both feen and felt in our unhappy Kingdom. The meaneft of Men, the bafeft and vileft of the Nation, the loweft of the People have got the Power into their Hands; trampled upon the Crown; baffled and mifufed the Parliament; violated the Laws; deftroyed or fuppreft the Nobility and Gentry of the Kingdom; opprefs'd the Liberties of the People in general; broke in funder all Bands and Tyes of Religion, Confcience, Duty, Loyalty, Faith, common Honefty, and good Manners; caft off all fear of God and Man; and now lord it over the Perfons and Eftates of all forts and ranks of Men from the King on his Throne, to the Beggar in his Cottage:

ma-

making their Will their Law ; their Power
their Rule ; their hairbrain'd giddy phana-
tical humour, and the setting up of a *Babel*
of Confusion, the end of all their Actions.
But how this misery is befallen us, the
Kingdom brought so low, and so unwor-
thily, unhappily, inconsiderately deliver'd
over into such base and ignoble hands, the
Parliament abused, betrayed, and now
become in show and in name the Instrument of their Tyranny, but in truth it self
made nothing ; and (if the presence of the
right Speaker be so essential to the being
and acting of a Parliament, and so necessary, that Sir *Edward Cook* says in his In-
stitutes the House cannot sit without him)
then is there clearly at this present no Parliament but an Assembly of Men, acted
and moved by the Art and Malice of some
few sitting among them, by the means of
an Army, which those few, those Vipers
of the Parliament, that have eaten out the
Bowels of their Parent and destroyed her,
raised (that is, abused the Parliament, making them raise it) under colour of necessity for the preservation of the Parliament
and Kingdom ; when in truth it was out
of a design to make themselves Masters of
both, that neither of them might ever enjoy Peace and Liberty more, to blast
our Hopes, nip all the fair Blossoms of
Re-

Reformation, dafh in funder all our preparations and endeavours for the eftablifh-
ing of a happy Peace ; and fo a glorious pro-
mifing Morning became a Day of darknefs,
a Day of treading down and perplexity :
this, I fay, will be worth the enquiry, and
perhaps be no difficult thing to difcover,
and make fo plain, that he who runs may
read.

2. Yet I would not be conceived to attribute fo much of Wifdom and Forefight to
thefe Men, as to believe they had laid this
whole Defign, with the feveral Circum-
ftances and Steps of proceeding from the
beginning ; which not the Devil himfelf
was fo politick and foreknowing as to have
done. But I am perfwaded that they had
it in their general Aim, and laid it as a foundation for all their Superftructures, to do
as much mifchief as they could, make the
Diforder as great, the Change as univerfal
as was poffible, and ftill to improve all opportunities, and occafions *ex re natâ*, putting on for more as they prevailed in any
thing, till at laft even beyond what either
they could hope, or we could fear, their
Defign was brought to this perfection, as
will appear by the fequel of this Difcourfe.

3. When in the beginning of this Parliament, in the Year 1642. after fome pro-
grefs in a Parliamentary way to the re-

lieving

lieving of many of our Grievances, and reforming many Abuses both in Church and State (for which we were not sufficiently thankful) it pleased God, in his just Judgment, for the punishment of our Sins, to send a Spirit of Division between the King and the Parliament, and things grew to that height, as both of them appealed to the Sword to plead their Cause, and decide their Quarrel; the Members of Parliament, who then engaged, declared themselves to desire nothing but the settlement of the Kingdom, in the honour and greatness of the King, and in the happiness and safety of the People: And whensoever that could be obtained, to lay down the Sword, and submit again to the King's Scepter of Peace more willingly than ever they resisted his Force and Power. This I am sure was the ultimate end of many, I may say, of the chiefest of those who at that time appeared: upon which principle they first moved, and from which they never departed; which made them at that time resolve to put their Lives into their hands, and offer them a Sacrifice to the welfare and happiness of their Prince and Country. I say Prince as well as Country, tho he perhaps look'd on them as his greatest Enemies; but they consider'd him as their Prince, whom Nature, Duty, the Command

mand of God, and the Laws of Men, obliged them to reverence, and to love as the Head and Father of the People ; whose greatnefs confifted in his People's, and his People's in his ; and therefore neither could be great, nor happy, one without the other, which made thofe faithful ones put them both in the fame Ballance, and rather adventure his difpleafure by promoting the publick Caufe, than (as they thought) his ruin by deferting it.

4. Whilft thefe Men acted in the fimplicity of their Hearts, there was another Generation of Men, which, like the frozen Snake that lay in their Bofoms, feemed to defire but the fame things with them, and that the fame fhould have contented them, when it was nothing fo ; but they had further Defigns, to deftroy and cut off not a few, to make the Land an *Aceldama*, ruin the King, and as many of the Nobility and Gentry as they could, alter the Government, have no order in the Church, nor power in the State over them. This was the Venom they harbour'd, which at firft they were not warm enough to put forth : But it foon appeared by fome evident Symtoms, which difcovered it to difcerning Eyes, though many were very long abufed. For as the Devil can transform himfelf into an Angel of Light ; fo they pretended

tended Zeal in Religion, and to be publick
Spirits, as if none were so holy and self-denying as they: and so insinuated themselves into the good Opinion of Men; and,
being bold and forward, got into all Im-
ployments, engrossed the whole managing
of the War (that is, the directive part
of it, not the fighting) whilst others, who
meant plainly, and honestly, went into
their several Countries, desirous to see the
business soon at an end; and, either by
shewing the Sword, to have kept it in on
both sides, or else, if God had otherwise
determin'd that some Blood must be drawn,
to adventure their own for speedy stopping
the issue of it in the Kingdom.

5. This was the first step of those unworthy Mens getting into power. When
other Gentlemen of the House of Commons unluckily left it upon these occasions, they then undertook the business, put
themselves and their Creatures into all
Committees, persons most of them before
only known by their Faces, and esteemed
for their Silence and Modesty. But they
soon grew Bold and Impudent, domineering not only over the rest of the House,
but much more over others abroad, and by
their Pride and Insolency contracting Envy and Hatred to the Parliament.

6. By this means they had power over all the Money of the Kingdom, pleafured and recompenfed whom they would, which were none, be fure, but their Creatures, or fuch as would be theirs; and fo made many Profelytes both within doors and without, increafing their Party exceedingly, which made them carry the bufinefs of the Houfe as they would themfelves: and made it eafie to them, in all Debates concerning applications for Peace, to drive us to extremities, demanding unreafonable things, laying upon the King the Conditions of *Naafh*, to thruft out his right Eye for a reproach; or, as the Devil did to our Saviour, to have him fall down and worfhip them, lay his Honour at their Feer, his Life at their Mercy; while they, upon all occafions, revile and reproach him, give countenance and encouragement to all the bitter, fcurrilous and unfeemly Expreffions againft him, impeach the Queen, give her the ufage (both in words and actions) one would not have done to the meaneft Handmaid of the Kingdom, tho the Wife, Daughter, and Sifter of a King, the Mother of our Prince, who is to fit upon the Throne, if thefe Men hinder him not; and all this, to make the diftance wide, the wound deep, that there might be no clofing, no binding up. Then was there

no-

nothing but expelling Members out of the House on the leaft information. If any of thofe Whelps did but bark againft any one, and could but fay he was bufie in the Country, nothing but fequeftring, impeaching of Treafon, turning Men and their Families, turning Wife and Children to ftarve : fo many Committees and Sub-Committees of Examinations, Sequeftrations, fifth and twentieth part, &c. made in City and Country, and fome of the moft factious, bufy, beggarly men put in, as fitteft Tools for fuch Mafters to work by, to rake Men to the Bones, and take all advantages to ruin them.

7. This was a great breaking of heart to all honeft Men, efpecially to thofe in the Houfe, who being prefent and Eye-witneffes of the management of Affairs, eafily difcovered the drift of thefe perfons, and oppofed it all they could : which made thofe Blood-fuckers conceive a mortal hatred againft them, and in truth againft all *Gentlemen*, as thofe who had too great an intereft, and too large a ftake of their own in the Kingdom, to ingage with them in their Defign of perpetuating the War to an abfolute confufion.

8. This made them look with a jealous Eye upon my Lord of *Effex*, who was General of the Army, finding him not fit for
their

their turn, as too defirous of Peace, and of
maintaining Monarchy; and therefore they
refolve to lay him afide, beginning to draw
Supplies from him, neither providing Re-
cruits, nor furnifhing him with Money or
Arms (except fometimes for a pinch, when
the neceffity of their own prefervation
required it) clogging him all they could,
countenancing and fupporting who ever
did oppofe him: In the mean time carrying
on the bufinefs of the Houfe in a wild madnefs, making Ordinances, like *Draco*'s
Laws, written in Blood, that no Man
could be fafe whom they had a mind to
deftroy, and their mind was to deftroy all
they could, by making fo many defperate,
to render things more irreconcileable, and
cut off all hopes of Peace, which they were
refolved to put by upon any terms, *per fas
aut nefas*, if not by art and cunning, rather
to ufe force than fail, and where the Fox's
Skin would not reach, to take the Lion's;
as to give one Inftance for all.

9. The Houfe of Lords in the Summer after the beginning of our Troubles in 1643,
having refolv'd to deliver themfelves and
the Kingdom from this *Ægyptian* Slavery,
had prepared a Meffage to the King, with
Overtures for an Accommodation, and fent
it down to the Houfe of Commons on a
Saturday, where the major part feemed to
be

be of the fame mind, and after a long difpute and much oppofition prevail'd to take it into confideration, made an entrance into it, agreed to fome particulars, and it growing late, adjourned the further debate till Monday morning ; againft which time thefe Firebrands had fet the City in a flame, as if there were a refolution to betray all to the King ; and thereupon brought down a Rabble of their party, fome thoufands to the Houfe of Commons door, who gave out threatning Speeches , and named among themfelves (but fo as they might be heard) fome Members of the Houfe, whom they faid they lookt upon as Enemies, and would pull out of the Houfe ; which did fo terrifie many honeft timorous Men, and gave that boldnefs to the others, as contrary to all order they refumed the Queftion that was fettled on Saturday for going on with the bufinefs, and at laft carried it by fome Voices to have it laid afide : which was the higheft ftrain of Infolency, the greateft violation of the Authority and Freedom (the two effential Ingredients) of a Parliament that before that time was ever known. Since, I confefs, the Army has far outftrip'd it.

10. This made fome perfons caft about how a ftop might be given to fuch violent proceedings, and to have other Counfels ad-

admitted, which probably would give some allay to thofe fharp and implacable Spirits : It appearing to be altogether impoffible e-ver to obtain a Peace, whilft they were Ru-lers, who *Phaeton* like, were able to fet the whole World on fire. It was therefore propofed that our Brethren of *Scotland* might be called in, who were known to be a wife People, lovers of Order, firm to Monarchy : who had twice before gone through the misfortune of taking up Arms, and wifely had laid them down ; ftill con-tenting themfelves with that which was neceffary for their fecurity, avoiding ex-tremities. Their wifdom and modera-tion, as was prefumed, might then have delivered us from that precipice of mifery and confufion, into which our Charioteers were hurrying us amain.

11. But thefe Men would none of it at that time ; they hoped to be able to carry on the Work themfelves, and meant to di-vide all the Spoil : which they had done if it had not pleafed God to give them that check in the Weft, when their Army there was beaten through Sir *Arthur Haflerig*'s default, one of their invincible Champi-ons. Firft, his ignorant foolhardinefs, af-terwards his bafenefs and cowardife, who then found himfelf to be mortal (for before he thought himfelf invincible, and abfolutely

lutely Stick-free and Shot-free, having had the good Fortune to be in a gallant Regiment, under Sir *William Balfore*, at *Kenton*-Field, and so not to run away) but, as himself did afterwards relate it, wink and strike, and bear down all before him. This made him so absolute a Souldier, as he thought Christendom had not his fellow, and therefore would not be govern'd by his Commander in chief, in that Western Brigade, a gallant and discreet Gentleman; but would charge contrary to order, without sense or reason: and, finding that resistance which he did not expect, ran away as basely with all the Horse, leaving the Foot engaged. Presently afterwards the Town of *Bristol* was lost by the like Gallantry and good Soldiery of another of their Champions, who for it was condemned to die by a Council of War, and pardoned by my Lord of *Essex*, who was well requited for it afterwards both by this Gentleman and his Father.

12. Then our Masters, finding themselves to be mortal too, began to be afraid; and now the *Scots* must be called in. So in all hast they send to them to come and help, with open Cry, *Save us, or we perish*. They promise any thing, offer any thing, do any thing for the present that the *Scots* would have them do: The Honour of *England*

land not thought of, Liberty of Confcience and the godly Party not mentioned : But all that was heard was the Covenant, Uniformity in Church-Government, uniting the Nations, never to make Peace without them, and a folemn Treaty for all this clofed there, and prefently ratified by the Parliament here.

13. But they meant afterwards to be even with them, to perform nothing of what was *de futuro* to be done, to ferve their turns by them, to make them inftrumental for their deliverance at that plunge, and then pick quarrels with them and fend them home again with fcorn and difcontent, which they have fince fufficiently laboured to do, and went far towards it, and to the engaging of the two Kingdoms in Blood ; if fome perfons had not interpofed with more ingenuous and more moderate Counfels, to the happy fuccefs of whofe Endeavours the piety, honefty, and moderation of the *Scots* themfelves did very much contribute, concurring with them, and cooperating in all things which might promote a Peace, as fhall be afterwards fhewed in its due place : for this is but by the way.

14. Thofe Creatures of theirs whom they fent Commiffioners into *Scotland* for that

bu-

buſineſs, repreſented the ſtate of Affairs to
that Parliament clear otherwiſe than it .
was, endearing their own Party to them
as the only ſincere publick ſpirited Men,
who deſired ſuch a Reformation as was a-
greeable to their Government, and ſuch a
Peace as might be a joint ſafety and ſecurity to both Kingdoms, giving Characters of
all others as Malignants, ill affected, averſe
to the Scotiſh Nation, oppoſers of a good
underſtanding between the Kingdoms, and
of their mutual aſſiſtance of each other.

15. With which prejudice of us the
Scots were ſtrongly poſſeſſed, at their coming in about *January*, 1643. and were in
England ſome time before they were diſa-
buſed. They were firſt made believe nothing ſhould be done without them, or
their advice and conſent. To that purpoſe
a Committee of the two Kingdoms muſt be
appointed for uniting the Councils, to order and direct the proſecution of the War,
and for communicating and tranſacting all
Affairs between the Kingdoms : In pack-
ing whereof, and keeping out ſome perſons whom our Maſters did diſaffect, they
uſed ſuch juggling, as never was heard of
before in Parliament, and none but ſuch
Hocus-pocus's could have the Face to have
done.

16. Well,

16. Well, they carried it, and to work they go, bearing it very fair to the *Scots*, till they were got aloft again, and that with their help they had recovered and cleared the North, obtained that great Victory at *Marston-Moor*, in *July* 1644, which without them they had never done. And however Lieutenant General *Cromwel* had the impudence and boldnefs to affume much of the honour of it to himfelf, or rather, *Herod* like, to fuffer others to magnifie him and adore him for it (for I can fcarce believe he fhould be fo impudent to give it out himfelf, fo confcious as he muft be of his own bafe cowardlinefs) thofe who did the principal Service that day, were Major General *Lefley*, who commanded the Scots Horfe, Major General *Crawford* who was Major General to the Earl of *Manchefter*'s Brigade, and Sir *Thomas Fairfax*, who, under his Father, commanded the Northern Brigade. But my friend *Comwel* had neither part nor lot in the bufinefs : For I have feveral times heard it from *Crawford*'s own mouth (and I think I fhall not be miftaken if I fay *Cromwel* himfelf has heard it from him ; for he once faid it aloud in *Weftminfter-Hall*, when *Cromwel* paft by him, with a defign he might hear him) that when the whole Army at *Marston-Moor* was in a fair poffibility to be utterly

terly

terly routed, and a great part of it run-
ning, he faw the Body of Horfe of that
Brigade ftanding ftill, and to his feeming
doubtful which way to charge, backward
or forward, when he came up to them in
a great paffion, reviling them with the
name of Poltroons and Cowards, and asked
them if they would ftand ftill and fee the
Day loft ? Whereupon *Cromwel* fhewed
himfelf, and in a pitiful Voice faid, Major General, what fhall I do? he (begging
pardon for what he faid, not knowing
he was there, towards whom he knew his
diftance as to his Superiour Officer) told
him, Sir, if you charge not all is loft ;
Cromwel anfwered, he was wounded, and
was not able to charge (his great wound
being a little burn in the Neck by the acci-
dental going off behind him of one of his
Soldiers Piftols) then *Crawford* defired him
to go off the Field, and fending one away
with him (who very readily followed
wholefom advice) led them on himfelf,
which was not the duty of his Place, and
as little for *Cromwel's* Honor, as it proved to be much for the advancement of
his and his Parties pernicious Defigns.
This I have but by relation, yet I eafily
believe it upon the Credit of the Re-
porter, who was a Man of Honor, that
was not afhamed nor afraid to publifh it in
all

all places. Befides, I have heard a parallel Story of his Valour from another perfon (Colonel *Dalbier*) not inferiour, neither in quality nor reputation, to Major General *Crawford*, who told me, That when *Bafing-Houfe* was ftorm'd, *Cromwel*, inftead of leading on his Men, ftood a good diftance off, out of Gun-fhot behind a Hedg. And fomething I can deliver of him upon my own knowledg, which makes paffage for the eafier belief of both thefe Relations, and affures me that that Man is as errand a Coward, as he is notorioufly perfidious, am-bitious, and hypocritical. This was his bafe keeping out of the Field at *Keinton* Battel; where he with his Troop of Horfe came not in, impudently and ridiculoufly affirming, the day after, That he had been all that day feeking the Army and place of Fight, tho his Quarters were but at a Village near hand, whence he could not find his way, nor be directed by his Ear, when the Ordnance was heard, as I have been credibly informed, 20 or 30 Miles off; fo that certainly he is far from the Man he is taken for.

17. That day's work at *Marfton-Moor* turned the Scales, and raifed again the fortune of the Parliament, which till that day had very much declined: And thefe Men (who all this while ftalked under the

C   fides

sides of the Parliament, and did but pretend the business of Reformation, and the Peoples Liberties, thereby to break the power of the King first, that afterwards they might, either by artifice or force, lay as low the Authority of Parliament, unless it would betray its truth, and yield to be instrumental to them) did, after this, begin to put out their Horns, appear in their Colours, and, as they warmed more and more, to spit out their Venom against Monarchy, against Nobility and Gentry, against that Reformation with which they had formerly held forth to the *Scots,* against the very Covenant, their Vows and Declarations wherewith they had abused God and the World.

18. Then did *Cromwel* declare himself to the Lord of *Manchester,* and indeed reveal'd the whole Design. First, His rancor against the *Scots,* as that he would as soon draw his Sword against them as against any of the King's Party. Then his hatred of the Nobility and House of Peers, wishing there was never a Lord in *England,* and saying, he loved such and such because they loved not Lords, and that it would not be well till he was but Mr. *Montague.* Thirdly, His intentions to hinder Peace, and that therefore he desired none to be of that Army, but such as were of the Independent judg-

judgment, to interpose if a Peace were like to be made which agreed not with their humours. All this remains upon Record in both Houses, being the Earl of *Manchester's* Charge against him. And let any one judg if this be not the very Plot which was then laid and since practised. Has not every particular been attempted by them? have they not fully compleated that which was chiefly aimed at? As that which will, and must certainly (if not prevented) bring on all the rest the hindering of Peace, that no ease nor quietness might be restored to the Kingdom. For when the Parliament was ready to disband the only Army then left, and so to free the Subject from all Payments and Taxes, that every one might return to his Vocation; and all differences between King and Parliament might be ended and reconciled in a parliamentary way; then did the *Cadmean* Brood turn their Swords against their fellow Subjects, and their Masters the Parliament, which by open force they assault, make void, and unvote what they had voted concerning their Disbanding, put by all thoughts of Peace, and throw back the Kingdom, which was entring into the desired Haven of Peace and Happiness, into the deep Seas of Storms and Misery and Confusion, where I beseech God it perish not: But of all this anon.

19. Things were not yet ripe; tho the Serpent's Eggs were laid by him in the Earl of *Manchester's* bosom, it was not time to hatch the Cockatrice. Therefore when it was by the Earl made known to the Houses, their Party in the House of Commons did (*more solito*) with all the violence and injustice in the world smother and suppress it, quarrelling that the Lords had infring'd their Privileges, in desiring that might be examined by a Committee in both Houses, saying, The Lords ought not to meddle in it, because it concern'd a Commoner; whereas nothing was more ordinary throughout the whole proceeding of this Parliament in all their inquisitions. Yet by that means this was then stifled, the breach of Privilege refer'd to a Committee of the House of Commons, and there the business died.

20. After this the *Scots* saw how they were cheated, and it came to be, though not an open breach, yet a great coldness between them, a withdrawing of confidence, of familiarity, of Counsels. And the *Scots* then found that the other party had been misrepresented, being the Men who, in truth, did agree with them in Principles and in Design: Which was only to reform, not to alter; to regulate, and so to save, not to destroy. That they still carried about with them the sense of their Allegiance

ance and Duty to the perfon of the King, whom they did defire to fee reinvefted into his Throne and Kingly Government, with fuch a power, and in fuch a way, as might be good both for Him and the People, that thereby confufion, mifery, and that difor-der which the Poet defcribes to have been in the firft Chaos, and which we now fee (not in a Fiction, but really feel and fmart under) might be avoided.

21. By little and little the *Scots* and thefe latter came to a better underftanding; at laft they difcover the horrid Practices and the whole Defign of the others, who, in the mean time, drove it on, *Jehu* like, vi-olently bearing down, and deftroying all that oppofed them; for fome oppofition they found. They faw there was a ftrong Party in the Houfe againft them, between whom and the Soldiers who were under Command of my Lord of *Effex*, there was a good Correfpondency; and thefe two, together with the *Scots*, were as a threefold Cord not to be broken by them: therefore they would untwift it, and fo deftroy them one after another.

22. The Earl of *Effex* muft be the firft who they found would not bow, and there-fore muft break; for many applications had been made to fee if he would ftoop to their Lure. Great offers, large promifes, all the

glory of the Kingdom fhould be his, if he would but worfhip them, be (as they termed it) true to the Godly Party: but he was true to his Principles. Therefore they do what they can to make him odious, not paying his Army, to make it a Burden to the Country, and infamous; not giving him means of acting by Supplies and Provifions, fo to be looked upon as a Drone or worfe, or putting him upon fuch Actions as fhould break him, fo to make him come off with difhonour.

23. As when he was about *Oxford* in the Summer 1644, he on one fide of the River, and Sir *William Waller* with his Brigade on the other; the King having then but a fmall force within the Town, and either not provided for a Siege, or not willing to be fhut in with a light body of Horfe, and I think fome mounted Men, held them play and diftracted them, being fometimes on the one fide, fometimes on the other; which was eafie for him to do, going through the Town, as he faw occafion, by the conveniency of the Gates: It being then known that he waited but his opportunity and advantage to flip by, or break through, our Grand Mafters ordered my Lord of *Effex*, with a heavy body of an Army and a great train of Artillery, to attend his Majefties motion, and Sir *William Waller* to go

into

into the Weſt, which they conceived would be an eaſie Task at that time to reduce the King's Party brought low, and ſo not able to ſend any Forces into thoſe parts for their relief and encouragement.

24. This they knew would abſolutely break my Lord of *Eſſex*, who muſt haraſs his Army to follow a light and moving Body; and if the King, which was probable enough, ſhould chance to give him the ſlip, and get from him into the Weſt, then was he ruin'd in his Reputation, and liable to a Queſtion, and perhaps a further Proſecution. It proved that his Majeſty did get by them, and paſſed by Sir *William Waller's* Quarters on the other ſide, who, as ſoon as he knew it, marched after him, and gave notice to my Lord of *Eſſex* thereof; ſo as before he knew any thing, Sir *William Waller* was got a days march before after the King. Then was it impoſſible for him to overtake them; and, being ſo much nearer the Weſt, Sir *William Waller* engaged in the other Service, he, upon the Advice of his Council of War, reſolved to bend that way, yet not to make ſuch ſpeed, but that he ſhould receive other Orders from our Governors above, that he might comply with them. Accordingly he gave that Account to the Parliament and Committee of the two Kingdoms, with his deſire of their Directions.

They

They were so mad to see themselves defeated of their Plot, that they would not for many days return him any answer at all; his disobedience was blown up, and trumpeted about by them and their Agents: Some of whom did not stick to say, It were better my Lord of *Essex* and his whole Army were lost and ruined, than the Parliament not obeyed, and, that by their consents, he nor his Army should be look'd after or cared for more: A Maxim they have forgotten now in the case of Sir *Thomas Fairfax* and his Army's, not Disobedience but open Rebellion; but they were as good as their words then, and did most maliciously, wilfully, and treacherously (as to the Parliaments Cause, which they seemed to be zealous in) suffer General and Army to be lost, and the whole West left further out of the Parliaments reach than before.

25. Sir *Arthur Haslerig* posted up to *London*, breathing out nothing but ruin and destruction to the Earl of *Essex*, spoke it out in the hearing of several persons, That he would ruin him, or be ruined himself. His malice and violence was so great at the Committee of the two Kingdoms, where he and his Party were prevalent, that a report was thence brought down to the House of Commons, by which Sir *William Waller* was taken off from following the King, and by

by that means the King was left at liberty
to bend his whole force for the Weft after
my Lord of *Effex*, which he prefently did.
At laft they left my Lord of *Effex* at liberty
to proceed in that Weftern Expedition, but
with a refolution to let him perifh. He
takes in *Weymouth* and fome other Towns,
goes on as far as *Cornwal*, whither the
King's Forces follow him at the heels, cut
off all provifion from him, prefs upon him
exceedingly, and put him to very great
ftreights. He engaged in a Country inclo-
fed with deep Ditches and ftrong Fences,
that he could neither break through, nor
march away; but fends Letter upon Letter, Meffenger upon Meffenger to the Parliament, reprefenting his Condition, and
how eafie it was with a fmall force fent upon the back of the King's Army, if but only a good Party of Horfe, to ftop their
Provifions, and turn the Tables, ftreighten
them and free him, than which certainly
nothing had been more eafie, and would
have faved the Kingdom a Mafs of Treafure, and thoufands of good Mens lives,
which the continuance of the War after that
time did coft.

26. But our Mafters did not defire then
to fee the War at an end; they had not the
Sword in thofe hands they would have it
for to break the King's forces, well knowing

ing they muft then have had a Peace, and fuch a Peace as had carried with it an eftablifhment of the King's Government, a keeping up the Nobility and Gentry; all things muft have returned into their proper Channel, and (the fecurity of the Parliament and Kingdom being provided for) the Law of the Land muft have taken place, their Arbitrary Empire been at an end, and their Defign wholly defeated.

27. Therefore my Lord of *Effex* muft not be relieved, but facrificed to their Ambition, the King's Army muft be yet preferved, to give them a colour to new model theirs, and put the Power into the bafe hands of their Creatures which fhould keep the Kingdom in a perpetual Bondage; and tho they ended the War with the King, yet never made Peace, but continued to grind the Faces and break the Backs of the People with Taxes and Free-Quarter, to maintain an Army when no Enemy was left; in a word, they govern by the Sword, the height of all Mifery and Slavery that any Land can undergo.

28. My Lord of *Effex* and his Army were by this means broken in *Cornwal* in the latter end of that Summer, and the King feemed to gain a great Advantage, recover a great deal of Strength; but to nip that, they foon provided Force fufficient, it fuiting
ing

ing with their Ends, that his Majesty should seem strong, but not be so. Therefore the Soldiers of that Army which had lost their Arms in *Cornwal* are presently armed again, and two other Armies joined to them, the Earl of *Manchester*'s and Sir *W. Waller*'s, who gave the King's Forces a ruffle at *Dennington*, gaining some of the Works : Yet, when the King came with the remainder of his Strength, they did not think it convenient to put it to the trial of a Day, but suffered him to march away, when it had been a most easie thing to have prevented it : And even there, in all likelyhood, have made an end of the business, which was that they feared ; and Sir *Arthur Haslerig* could come up to *London*, and into the House of Commons, all in beaten Buff, cross girt with Sword and Pistols as if he had been killing his thousands, when 'tis more probable, if there was any danger, that he had been crying under a Hedg, as he did at *Cherrington* Fight, bellowing out, *Ah wo is me, all is lost ! we are all undone !* insomuch that a great Officer, a Scotch-man, finding him in that tune, wished him to go off the Field, and not stand *gudding* there (a Scotch term for crying) to dishearten the Soldiers : but in the House of Commons he feared nothing, none so fierce and valiant, without fear or wit ; and there, like a great Soldier in that habit, gave a Relation of what

what had pass'd, highly extolling the gallantry and conduct of all the Commanders,
the valour of the Soldiers, that no mortal
Men could do more, that the best Soldiers
in the world could not have hinder'd the
King's marching off, and that it had been
no wisdom to have adventur'd to fight, for
that the King would be King still, and
would soon have had another Army, tho they
had gotten the better, but if he had beaten
them, they had been utterly lost. This served the turn for that time, to cast a mist
before the peoples eyes, and stop their
mouths. Yet within very few Weeks
after, this worthy Knight forgot all he
had said: for it is by *Cromwel* laid as a Crime
to the Earl of *Manchester*'s Charge (whom
they then meant to lay aside) that he was the
cause they fought not with the King, and
Sir *Arthur* is a principal Witness to make it
good. But on the other side, the Earl of
Manchester returns the Bill, charging *Cromwel*, that it was his not obeying Orders, who
being commanded as Lieutenant General of
the Horse, to be ready at such a place by
such an hour early in the Morning, came
not till the Afternoon, and by many particulars makes it clear to have been only his
fault.

29. And to say the truth, they could not
else have carried on their Design of new mo-
delling

delling their Army, of which then there had been no need, and preventing a Peace which they feared might elfe have followed. For if the King had been too fore preft at that time, it was in their apprehenfions probably he might have laid hold upon the Propofitions for Peace, which were then ready, and fent to him to *Oxford* immediately after.

30. Therefore now they fet upon their great Work, projected long before, and which *Cromwel* had broken to my Lord of *Manchefter* in the time of his greatnefs with him, when he thought him to be one of their own, that was to have an Army compofed of thofe of the Independent Judgment, to interpofe if there were like to be a Peace; only their Prefumption and Impudence was fwell'd to be fo much higher, as now, they would have no other Army but of them. Becaufe they faw the danger was over; there being no Enemy to take the Field againft them, but fuch an one as they had willingly fet up and given time and means to get together: fo as there would be no great need of fighting, that part having been acted by others; for they were never good at it, but excellent to affume the praife and reap the benefit, when others had done the work.

31. There-

31. Therefore the whole force of the Kingdom muſt be theirs, in the hands of their Creatures; all the Noblemen and Gentlemen who had engaged in the beginning, and born the heat of the day, muſt be laid by, all theſe gallant Officers who had done the Parliament the beſt Service, indeed all, muſt be caſhier'd : The Earl of *Eſſex*, the Earl of *Mancheſter*, Sir *Philip Stapleton*, Sir *William Waller*, and the reſt muſt be reduced, caſt by as old Almanacks, in truth not fitted to their Meridian.

32. For this Feat the Juggle of a Self-denying Ordinance is found out, whereby it is ordained, that no Member of either Houſe ſhall bear any Office Martial or Civil; which ſtrikes them all out of Employment and *Cromwel* too, but for him they will ſoon find a Starting-hole.

33. Then there muſt be one body of an Army compoſed of ſo many thouſand Horſe and Foot out of the ſeveral Armies, which were to be reduced (as I remember ſome 20 or 21 thouſand, which number they have ſince doubled or trebled for the eaſe of the Kingdom) the Officers to be named by the Houſe, and a Committee appointed under the ſpecious name of a Committee of Reformation for this Work, by which they tear in ſunder all their Forces, diſcontent all their beſt Officers and Soldiers, utterly diſ-
joynt

joynt the whole Frame of the Martial part of their Affairs, and, I dare say, put the King's Party in greater hopes of being able to make it good by the Sword, and less to apprehend the Consequence of not making a Peace at that time, than the gaining of a Battel would have done : nor in truth could it have any other Operation with rational Men.

24. So to work they go, and find difficulties enough. The Soldiers bore an affection to their old Officers, which made them unwilling to be reduced : Money there was not to give any reasonable satisfaction out of their Arrears to those who were to be cashier'd : But a fortnights pay was ordered, where many months were owing. Yet such was the obedience of those Officers (gallant Men, old Soldiers most of them) to the authority of Parliament (so unlike to the late rebellious Carriage and Insolency of our new Model, as shall be hereafter shewed) that they submit to it, are content to sit down themselves, and (which is more) use their interest to perswade the Soldiers to a Conformity. Some of the Horse who had served under my Lord of *Essex* were a little stiff, and made some shew of standing out in *Hertfordshire*, which our violent bloody new Modellers would have made advantage of presently to have faln on them,

them, and put them to the Sword; but the
Parliament followed more moderate Counsels, endeavouring to gain them through fair
means, by sending down some of their old
Officers to dispose them to a submission,
which employment they declined not, but
went and prevailed : to which my Lord of
Essex himself contributed very much, an
Example that this present young General
Sir *Thomas Fairfax* would not follow when
his Army was to be disbanded.

35. Yet such was the wickedness and desperate madness of those Men, who thirsted
after nothing but blood, mischief and confusion, that at the very same time when the
Parliament was going a gentle way, Mr. *St.
John* the King's Solicitor (one who I think
has as much of the Blood of this Kingdom
to answer for, and has dipp'd as deep in
all cunning pernicious Counsels, as any one
man alive) wrote a Letter under-hand to the
Committee of *Hertfordshire* (which is yet
extant) that they should raise the Country
and fall upon these men, to put all into
blood, contrary to the desire and endeavour
of the Parliament. A Villany never to be
forgotten nor forgiven in any man, much
less a Man of Law, who should better know
what price the Law sets upon the life of e-
very Subject, much more of many together, and of a whole County, which, if
he

he had been obeyed, had run a great hazard.

36. But I wonder not at this or any other such paſſage from him, who could have the face to ſay in his Argument againſt my Lord of *Strafford*, That ſome perſons were not to have Law given them, but be knockt on the head, no matter how; tho he knows it, or ſhould know it, to be againſt the Laws both of God and Man, that any ſhould be put to death before a legal Conviction, however he may have practiſed the contrary ſince the beginning of theſe unhappy troubles: his compoſition being, it ſeems, like that Monſter Emperor's *Lutum Sanguine maceratum.* And to leſs than an Emperor I would not parallel him, whoſe vaſt thoughts have carried him above King and Parliament, to frame, new mould, alter, and deſtroy as he thinks good. This mixture in his nature makes his actings ſo fierce and cruel. I appeal to all who have ſeen and obſerv'd him this whole Parliament, if, on all occaſions, his Opinion did not ſtill conclude *in ſeveriorem partem*; if he ever ſtopt where there was any way to it before he came to blood, or to the deſtruction of Eſtate and Fortune: But let him paſs.

37. To return to our buſineſs: Thoſe Soldiers were by theſe means perſwaded,

and

and the new Army framed, Colonels and o-
ther new Officers appointed, and for a Commander in chief Sir *Thomas Fairfax* is
found out ; one, as Sir *Arthur Haflerig* said,
as if he had been hew'd out of the Block for
them, fit for their turns to do whatever
they will have him, without confidering or
being able to judg whether honourable or
honeft. In the paffing his Commiffion
they made the firft plain difcovery of their
Intentions concerning the Perfon of the
King : for with a great deal of violence and
earneftnefs they preft it, and carried it, that
the care of the prefervation of his Perfon
fhould be left out, and that this Army fhould
go out in the name of the Parliament alone,
and not of King and Parliament, as it was
before under my Lord of *Effex*, who otherwife would not have medled with it. But
this General made no Bones, took it, and
thanked them, refolved (as it feems) to do
whatfoever thofe his Mafters fhould bid
him : for I'm fure he has, at their command, led his Army fince againft the Parliament, which he feemed to adore above all
things upon Earth.

38. The next work was how again to
get in my friend *Cromwel*; for he was to
have the power, Sir *Thomas Fairfax* only
the name of General ; he to be the Figure,
the other the Cypher. This was fo grofs
and

and diametrically againſt the letter of the Self-denying Ordinance, that it put them to ſome trouble how to bring it about. For this *Cromwel's* Soldiers, forſooth, muſt mutiny, and ſay they will have their *Cromwel* or they will not ſtir. Hereupon he muſt be ſent down; no word then of cutting or hewing, or of forcing them to a ſubmiſſion, as in the caſe of the Earl of *Eſſex's* Soldiers; but they muſt have their wills. Yet for theſe very men had *Cromwel* undertaken before, when upon debate the inconveniency was objeſted which might follow by diſcontenting the common Soldiers, who would hardly be drawn to leave their old Officers and go under new, he could ſay, that his Soldiers had learn'd to obey the Parliament, to go or ſtay, fight or lay by the Sword upon their command; which I know prevail'd with a great many to give their Vote with that Ordinance.

39. By this trick a little beginning was made towards the breach of it, which was ſoon made greater. For they cauſed a report to be ſpread, That the King was bending with his Forces towards the Iſle of *Ely*, but none could ſave but *Cromwel*, who muſt be ſent in all haſte for that Service, and an Order of diſpenſation is made for a very few Months, two or three (I remember not well whether) but with ſuch proteſtations of that

Party,

Party, that this was only for that Exigency, and that for the World they would not have the Ordinance impeached, as Mr. Sollicitor faid ; and that if no body would move for the calling him home at the expiration of that time, he would. But all this was to gull the Houfe. Mr. Sollicitor had forgot his Protestation, and before that was out there is another Order for more Months, and fo renewed from time to time, that at laft this great Commander is riveted in the Army, and fo faft riveted, as after all his Orders of continuance were at an end, he would keep his Command ftill, which he has done for feveral Months, and dos yet, not-withftanding that Ordinance, without any Order at all of the Houfe for it.

40. There, now they have the Sword where they would have it, and refolve with it to cut all Knots they cannot untie ; yet they defire to keep that Refolution behind the Curtain as long as they could, and would be thought very obedient to the Par-liament, hoping they fhould be always able to have it carried there according to their mind ; and partly by the awe of their Pow-er, partly by hopes of reward and advan-tage, ftill to have the major Vote. Which was eafie for them, having both Sword and Purfe, and withal an impudence and bold-nefs to reward all thofe who would fell their

Con-

Confciences. For all fuch Members of the
Houfe, and others were fure to be prefer'd,
have large Gifts given them out of the
Commonwealth's Money, Arrears paid, Offices confer'd upon them, countenanced and
protected againft all Complaints and Profe-
cutions, had they done never fo unworthy,
unjuft, horrid actions, to the oppreffion of
the Subject, and difhonour of the Parliament. All others difcountenanc'd, oppos'd,
inquifitions fet upon them, queftion'd, imprifon'd upon the leaft occafion, colours of
Crimes many times for doing real good Service, and no favour nor juftice for them : Only that the World might fee which was the
way to rife, and which to be fure to meet
with contrary Winds and Storms, and fo
to make all men at leaft to hold Candles to
thefe vifible Saints.

41. But a Party in the Houfe ftill troubled them, which faw their Juglings, their
under-hand dealings, fufpected their Defigns, found what they drove at, and coun-
termin'd them, oppos'd them, fometimes
croft and defeated their Practices, always
vext them, and did, in a great meafure, di-
vert and keep off Evil, tho the ftream
was fo ftrong they could not attain and effect the Good they defir'd.

42. This knot muft be broken, and fome
of the perfons removed, who are reprefent-

ed to the Kingdom by thefe Men and their
Agents, as thofe who were rotten at heart,
not faithful to the Parliament, holding correfpondence and intelligence with the King.
This was upon Generals, only to prepare
Mens minds to make paffage for an approbation of any attempts to their prejudice,
and give credit to fuch Lies and falfe Accu-
fations as they fhould be able to fet on foot:
and all means are us'd to procure Witneffes
to teftifie any thing againft them, Prifoners
examin'd and encourag'd to fay fomething,
any fcandalous defperate Rogues receiv'd
and hearken'd to, Spies fet to watch them,
their goings out and comings in, what places they went to, what perfons they vifited
or that vifited them. Some of their Agents
confeft they have been two years together
watching about fome of our Houfes, yet it
pleafed God to protect the Innocent, and,
notwithftanding all thefe endeavours, it was
never in their power to do any great mifchief in this bafe unworthy way.

43. They came neareft to their Mark,
when they had gotten the Lord *Savil*, a
known infamous Impoftor, to accufe me
with keeping correfpondence with my Lord
Digby (of which he faid he had notice given
him by a Letter in Cypher from the Dutch-
efs of *Buckingham*) and for what I did and
faid at *Oxford*, when I was amongft others
　　　　　　　　　　　　　　　　fent

fent thither to prefent Propofitions to the
King, where they had a fit Inftrument to
act for them, and fay and fwear any thing
they would have him, who was at that very time employed by fome of their principal ones, to truck and drive a Treaty under-
hand with fome great perfons at *Oxford*.
For the chief among them had always Grace
to try more ways than one to the Wood,
and commonly not to row the way they
look'd, willing enough to have made a
good bargain for themfelves at Court, and
then have left their Whelps, their Zealots, to
have mended themfelves as they could, perhaps not defpairing but to have perfwaded
them it was for their good, and the advancement of their Catholick Caufe, fo to have
quieted them, and fome little thing fhould
have been done for their fatisfaction. I did
with my own Eyes fee Letters, and fo did
feveral perfons, Members of both Houfes,
fome yet alive, fome dead, witten by *Savil*
to divers of great quality at *Oxford*, one to
L. D. fome to others, with only one Letter
for their Names, where intelligence was given of the proceedings and intentions of the
Parliament and their Army, many Propofitions made in the name of that Party and
their Undertakings, and in the Clofe my
Lord *Savil* to be Lord Treafurer, Mr. Solicitor to be Lord Keeper, and others of their

D 4   Fa-

Faction to have several Offices of Honour and
Trust. These Letters were seen likewise by
my Lord *Willoughby* and Mr. *Whitlock*, who
are yet alive, and can testifie it, and by the
Earl of *Essex*, Sir *Philip Stapleton*, and Sir
Christopher Wray, who are dead. Some of
them were written by *Savil's* own hand,
some copy'd out by a person of Honour, who
was employ'd by him, and is yet alive to
make it good : And when they play'd this
Game themselves, and pretended, forsooth,
a design upon *Oxford*, and to have the King's
Army in the West deliver'd to them (which
was all but collusion and deceit, to abuse the
World, and colour their Correspondencies)
then did they make *Savil* play the Villain
and accuse me, whom they prosecuted with
that height of malice and violence, with so
much injustice and partiality, especially that
Man of Law Mr. Sollicitor, who tho
Mr. *Whitlock* had not only consented to, but
joined in, and advised all that I had done at
Oxford, and that *Savil* himself had laid it e-
qually upon us both in his Information (it
seems either not so wicked as his setters on,
or not fully instructed by them) yet such
was the Justice of that Man, as he would
needs sever our Cases, and was not ashamed
not only so to declare his Judgment, but
press'd it and sollicited it, that the proceedings might be singly against me : whereby
the

the eyes of many indifferent perfons, Members of the Houfe, were open'd, and their Spirits rais'd to an Indignation, infomuch that in fpight of the Sollicitor and his Party, I was acquitted by the Houfe.

44. This made them bethink themfelves, begin to miftruft the Houfe, and doubt if they fhould be able to carry things as formerly: And thereupon refolve on a courfe, which fome amongft them had formerly ftill oppos'd or declin'd, as Mr. Sollicitor by name, which was to have the vacant places of thofe they had thruft out filled up by a new Election, iffuing out Writs for it under their new Great Seal. This they hoped would alter the Conftitution of the Houfe, and give them infallibly a majority of Votes. Accordingly in the long Summer Vacation of the year 1645, when very many of the Members were gone into their feveral Countries, they fall upon that point of recruiting the Houfe; and notwithftanding the thinnefs thereof, and its being furprifed with that Debate, their Creatures moft of them there (as they were always fure of fome fifty Voices, perfons whofe only Employment was there to drudg and carry on their Mafters work, having thereby a greatnefs far above the Sphere they had formerly mov'd in; whereas the others were Gentlemen, who had Eftates which requir'd their looking after,

ter, and all of them some Vocations, either
for their particular business or pleasure,
which made them less diligent, and many
of them, as at other times, so then away)
yet they carried it but by three Voices.

45. Then to work they go to canvass for
Elections in all places, for the bringing in
of such as should be wholly theirs. First,
they did all they could to stop Writs from
going any whither but where they were
sure to have fit Men chosen for their turns,
and many an unjust thing was done by them
in that kind : Sometimes denying Writs,
sometimes delaying till they had prepared
all things, and made it, as they thought,
cock-sure : Many times Committee-men in
the Country, such as were their Creatures,
appearing grossly, and bandying to carry
Elections for them ; sometimes they did it
fairly by the power of the Army, causing
Soldiers to be sent and quarter'd in the
Towns where Elections were to be, awing
and terrifying, sometimes abusing and offering violence to the Electors. And when
these undue Elections were complain'd of,
and question'd at the Committee of Privileges, there appeared such palpable partiality, so much injustice, such delays and tricks
to vex Parties grieved and their Witnesses,
such countenancing and defending those
who had done the wrong, as it dishearten'd
eve-

every body, and made many even fit down
and give over profecution.

46. Notwithftanding all this, and that
by this means fome perfons unduly chofen
were brought in, yet it prov'd, that far the
greater part of thofe new Members deceiv'd
the expectation of thefe Men. For tho
they came into the Houfe with as much prejudice as was poffible againft the other moderate Party, who had always been reprefented to them as perfons ill affected, not
faithful to the Parliament, obftructing all
bufineffes that were for the good of the
Kingdom, having Self-ends and ambitious
defigns of their own ; when they came to fit
in the Houfe themfelves, to fee with their
own eyes the carriage of things, underftand
the ways and drift both of the one and the o-
ther Party, difcern the tricks and violent
proceedings of the one, and plainnefs and
reality of the other ; that all thefe aimed at
was but to get a good Peace, fee the Government fettled both in Church and State, and
make no advantages to themfelves, have no
fhare, nor defir'd none of the Moneys, look
after no Offices nor Preferments; in a word,
not feek themfelves but the pulick; and thofe
on the other fide hinder and oppofe the fettling of the Government, and keep things in
a diftraction and confufion, not willing to put
up the Sword, but continue the burdens
and

and preſſures of the Country, countenance
the inſolencies of Soldiers, bear them out in
their abuſing of Miniſters, and other honeſt
Men, who were for Church-Government,
keep up factions and drive on intereſts in
the Houſe, put themſelves, their Kindred
and Friends into all places of power and profit, ſhare and divide among them the Com-
mon-wealth's Money, by Gifts and Re-
wards, and paying pretended Arrears; in a
word, ſeek the ruin of the Kingdom, and
the advancement of themſelves and their
Party; this made them change their Minds,
and many of them to confeſs and acknowledg they had been abuſed.

47. But this was not the work of one
day: Some time paſſed before they could
make theſe clear diſcoveries and diſabuſe
themſelves; our grand Impoſtors kept them
a good while at gaze, with putting jealou-
ſies into their heads againſt the *Scots*, as if
the *Scots* had a deſign of making good their
footing in this Kingdom, and that we who
were of the other Party from them did carry
on the Scotch Intereſt, and deſign'd to betray
the Rights and Liberties of *England*; with
which Engine they batter'd a long time, and
made no ſmall impreſſion in many mens
Minds.

48. For the next ſtep they meant to make,
was to fall foul with the *Scots*, and engage
the

the Kingdoms one againſt another in Blood, which was the return they would give the *Scots,* as a reward of the good Service they had done them, coming to their help in time of need, when they were ſo low, ſo deſpairing of carrying on their work, and effecting what they had projected to themſelves, as that the chief of them a little before were ready to run away, Ships prepared, good ſtore of Treaſure which they had ſhark'd, pack'd up to carry with them, or return'd beyond Sea by Bills of Exchange, and all things in a readineſs for their remove, ſo well were they reſolved to hazard, and (if need were) ſacrifice themſelves for their Country, tho they would be thought to be the only Patriots; but they had certainly left it in the lurch, if firſt my Lord of *Eſſex* had not done that memorable piece of Service in relieving *Gloceſter* (which was ſo gallantly defended by Major General *Maſſey*) and fighting the great Battel of *Newbury.* And a little before that the Kingdom of *Scotland* engaging in the Cauſe, ſent in their Army to their aſſiſtance. My Lord of *Eſſex,* as has been ſhewed already, had his reward; he was caſhier'd, and ſo was Major General *Maſſey,* who ſince likewiſe is turn'd out of the Houſe (being one of the eleven Members) and voted to be impeached of High Treaſon. And next the *Scots* muſt have
theirs.

theirs. The quarrelling with them, and endeavouring to deftroy their Army, is what I muft now fpeak of, as the Subject of the next Act in this Tragedy. The firft endeavour is to break the Scotifh Army, by not paying it, which before, whilft they had need of it, or hopes that the Kingdom of *Scotland* might cooperate to the working of their Defigns, they could be careful to do their utmoft to fatisfie, and to provide for it fitting Accommodations. But now they can let many months pafs without fending them any Money, or taking any care for their fupply, or fo much as affording them good words. One of thefe two effects they thought this would certainly produce, either the Soldiers to run away, perhaps mutiny, fo the Army disband and fall to pieces, or elfe live upon Free-quarters, fo by oppreffing the Country to become odious, and the people rife againft them. Nor were they wanting to give all encouragement fo to do; Emiffaries were fent out, and Agents employ'd in all places to ftir up and imbitter mens Spirits. Many Complaints were, by their procurements, fent up to the Parliament, and all means ufed to get hands to thofe Complaints, and ftrange things were fuggefted, vaft Sums to be levy'd by them, fo many thoufand Pounds a week to be levy'd upon a County, unheard of Infolencies

to

to be committed, Robbing, Killing, Ravishing, Riots, all manner of Villanies. This would come up with open cry, make a great noise, be received and heighten'd in the House of Commons with railing Speeches, bitter Invectives, blown over the City and Kingdom to the disadvantage and reproach not only of the Army, but the Nation; in a word, all done that could be imagin'd to set Man, Woman and Child, and even the very Stones against them. The Commissioners of *Scotland* that were in *London* would many times send in their Papers to the Houses of Parliament, to shew the falshoods of those Reports, and desire that Committees might be sent down to join with theirs to examine these things; pressing that it ought to be so done by the Treaty between the two Kingdoms, and that there should always be a Committee of both Kingdoms with the Army to govern it, to provide what was fit for the Soldiers, and prevent both disorders and misunderstandings: but it was not that which our Masters desir'd, and therefore they would send none.

49. The Members of the House who dislik'd those Courses, and saw the endeavours that were us'd to cause a breach between the two Nations, did yet desire, that if those relations were true, it might so appear, and be represented not only to the

Ge-

General of the Army, and to that part of the
Committee of Estates of *Scotland* which was
in *England* (both those with the Parliament
and those with the Army) but even to the
Kingdom of *Scotland*, that there might be
redress, the Offenders punish'd, and the
Kingdom of *England* righted and satisfy'd :
If false, that the raisers and contrivers of
those Reports might be punish'd, and the
Kingdom of *Scotland* repaired, which was
the way to keep Peace between the Nations.
And so sometimes they prevail'd, and got it
order'd for an Examination, but never any
thing could be made of it.   Only at a Mar-
ket-Town in *Yorkshire* there had been a
Riot, and some Men killed ; for which a
Council of War had passed on the Offenders,
and some (as I remember) were executed,
some cashier'd.   And for the raising those
great Sums of Money, it is true, Money they
did raise, or else their Soldiers must have
starv'd : But for that exorbitancy of raising
so many thousand Pounds a Week upon one
County, it was a Scandal and false Lye,
grounded upon notable Cheat and Collusion.
For the *Scots* drawing their Quarters near
together, which they did, as well for the
better governing of their Army, as for the
safety of it, knowing they had many back-
friends, this made them lie heavy upon
places, and exact the more Money and Provisions

vifions from thofe feveral Townfhips. Then
did thefe Men who were employed to blow
the Coals, and put all into a flame (if poffible) between the Country and the *Scots*, take
the higheft rate that was fet upon any one
of thefe Towns, and make a computation
what it would come to upon the whole
County at that proportion, which Sum they
inform'd to be the charge upon that County for the payment of the Scotifh Army;
and this muft be made a great bufinefs and
paft for a truth, as if the *Scots* had rais'd fo
much Money, when in truth there was no
fuch thing.

50. Yet let me not be thought to excufe
and juftifie all that the Soldiers of that Army
have done upon the Country, and not to
pity with a very tender Senfe, the deep Sufferings of thofe Northern parts, the Scotifh
Army lying fo long upon them on Free-
quarter. I muft be very ignorant of the
carriage of an unpaid Army, if I did not believe that many diforders were committed,
many a poor Country-man exceedingly opprefs'd and abus'd by the unruly Soldiers,
and more by half taken and fpoiled by them,
than would have fufficed for their Pay and
Entertainment, if it had been orderly raifed
and provided by the authority and care of the
State which was to pay them. And fo fhould
I likewife have very fmall bowels towards my

E   Coun-

Country, *England* in general, and particularly those poor Counties, in one of which I
receiv'd my being, if I did not grieve and
mourn from the bottom of my Soul for the
sad condition which did then overspread
them, the poverty to which they are] reduced, the ruin of so many Houses and Families, the Land lying in many places an unin-
habited Wilderness, all over a face of misery
and desolation. But then the more I am raised to an indignation against them who were
the cause of this, those who had rather suffer
not one County or two, but all the Counties in *England*, and two Kingdoms besides
to perish and ruin, than they to fail of their
Ends. So must all the North be made a Sacrifice to their malice and revenge upon the
Scotish Nation, and rather than not enforce
the *Scots* to oppress those parts, hoping at
last they would fall one upon another, they
will suffer the Country to endure any Misery; and not only so, but impudently and
perfidiously wrest and misinterpret the Treaty themselves had made, and so put a great
scorn thereon, to give greater provocations
to the *Scots* : and thus they make themselves
ridiculous and infamous to the World, and
to all posterity, by a gross and palpable collusion.

5t. For when the Commissioners of *Scotland* and the General of the Army did so often

ten and earneftly move for Pay for the Soldiers, reprefenting that on the monthly
Pay which was condition'd for and promi-
fed, they have not of fo many Months received any thing, and that it was impoffible to obferve that Difcipline in the Army
which was requifite for the eafe of the County, becaufe the Soldiers were unpaid, they
had the face to fay, that by the Treaty the
Scots could not receive their Pay at prefent,
becaufe there was a Claufe, that if any part
thereof were behind, they fhould be allow-
ed Intereft for forbearance (which Intereft
was not to be prefently paid neither, but afterwards when the Peace was fetled and the
Kingdom more able) upon which thefe
confcionable Logicians infer'd, that allow-
ing Intereft nothing could be demanded.
So that which the *Scots* gave way to out of
friendlinefs and confidence, to fhew they
would not exact upon our neceffities, if at
any time through the great occafions of expence we were not able to give them their
full Pay, is now made ufe of, and ungrate-
fully turned upon them, to defer the payment of any part : And this only to affront
them, and make them defperate.

52. And as they deal with the Army, fo
did they with the State and Kingdom of
Scotland, by putting neglects and indignities
upon their Minifters, raifing jealoufies of

them

them and of the whole Nation. For this
they had their *Robert Wright,* and their unknown Knight to give intelligence of Cor-
refpondencies held by them with the Queen,
of undertaking to do great matters for the
King, Treaties with *France,* ftrange defigns
and practices againft the Parliament, and e-
very foot Letters of Information from fome
well-wifhers abroad to Mr. Sollicitor, or Sir
Henry Mildmay, or fome other of that Gang,
upon this ftrain. Then this is whifper'd a-
bout, and thefe Letters go from hand to
hand, and told as a fecret in every bodies
Ears, to make people afraid and miftruft e-
ven their own Shadows, as if all were in
danger. Sometimes the Houfe muft be acquainted with fome of thefe things, or fome
perfon or other brought to the Bar to make
fome relation, as Sir *Thomas Hanmore.* Then
the doors are fhut, long winded Speeches
made to fet out our dangers, and great expectations rais'd of ftrange difcoveries, and all
but a *parturiunt montes.* Yet this ferves to
make a noife, and they had Inftruments abroad
to improve it, and many honeft well meaning
men were cozen'd and ftood at gaze, knew
not what to think of their Brethren of *Scotland*, nor yet of the Members of either
Houfe, and defir'd to have things more fairly carry'd towards them ; and as they had
had experience of their faithfulnefs formerly,

ly, so could they not be brought by such artifices to have an ill opinion of them without better grounds for it, and therefore differ'd in the entertainment they gave to those alarms, judging them false and causeless, accordingly expressing themselves, diverting and breaking the desperate thrusts which these men made, and were therefore decry'd as Scotish, malignant, and prejudged in all they did or said.

53. The malice against the *Scots* rests not here, it carries them to discover and manifest slighting and neglecting, and (that not sufficiently provoking) a violent injuring and affronting of them. First, they vouchsafe not to answer the Papers they put into the House, some not at all, none presently (as formerly they were wont to do) nor in any convenient time: but make them wait days, and weeks, and months, for a return to what the Commissioners present from the Kingdom of *Scotland*, or from themselves in the name of that Kingdom.

54. The Committee of the two Kingdoms is now no more in esteem, than (as they say) a Saint without a Holiday: That which before did manage all the great business, which was looked upon with so much reverence, even as a sacred thing, pray'd for in the Churches like the Lords in the Council, had all the trust, all the power, not on-

E 3 ly

ly in matters of War, which were wholly
left to them by the ordinance of their Conſtitution; but all other buſineſs of conſequence, as framing propoſitions for Peace,
and all Addreſſes to his Majeſty, all Nego-
tiations with foreign States, whatſoever did
in any high degree concern the Parliament
or Kingdom, was ſtill referred to them, and
what they did, paſſed for Law, was ſeldom
or never alter'd in the Houſe. But now the
Tide was turn'd, they had nothing to do.
Sir *Thomas Fairfax* was diſcharg'd of his
ſubordination to them, and left to himſelf,
to do as he ſaw cauſe with his Army.
They of the Committee, who were of that
Faction, ſeldom or never came to it; ſo
that the Commiſſioners of *Scotland*, and
the other Members of it, did come and attend three or four days one after another,
ſometimes oftner, to no purpoſe, and no
Committee could ſit for want of a number:
nay, they prevail'd ſo far, as now to vilifie
and ſhew their neglect or jealouſie of the
Scotiſh Commiſſioners. They would ſometimes get buſineſs referred to the Members
of both Houſes that were of that Committee, with their Excluſion.

55. To provoke them yet more, they
break through the Law of Nations, which
in all places in the World give protection to
publick Miniſters employed by any Prince
or

or State, so as neither their Servants or Goods, and especially not their Letters, which are of greater consequence, and more immediately concern the Honour and Interest both of their Masters and them, ought to be in any sort touch'd or stop'd; yet the Packets of the Commissioners of *Scotland* must be intercepted, and their Letters broke open. This done several times in a secret and private manner, the Letters suppressed and never heard of more, which was a great wrong and injury to that Kingdom; yet cannot be said to be an affront, because it was not avowed. But they have likewise done it openly and avowedly in a most insolent way: Once they set a Captain, one *Massey*, at the Guards by *London*, knowing the Commissioners were sending an Express into *Scotland*; and this Captain (who deserves to be made an Example for it, and his Masters too who set him to work) stops the Gentleman who was sent with the Packet, takes the very Letters they had written to the Committee of Estates, reads them, and keeps the Messenger Prisoner upon the Guard, which was the highest affront, the greatest violation of the publick Faith, the greatest scandal to all Princes, States, and even Societies of Men, the basest unworthiest dealing with a Nation, to whom we were engag'd by Amity, League, Cove-

nant,

nant, common Interest, and all Bonds of
Gratitude for the good we had receiv'd from
them, that ever was heard of, or read in a-
ny Story, or I think ever will be again.
Yet was this fellow, by the power and interest of these Men, protected in the House
of Commons: So far from being punish'd,
when the Scotish Commissioners made their
Complaint, that when the Lords had committed him for it, they made the House set
him at liberty, and quarrel with the Lords
for breaking their Privileges, in committing
one who was under examination of their
Committee: for they had refer'd the business to a Commitee, in truth not to do
the Kingdom of *Scotland* any right in pu-
nishing the Offender, but affront it the more
in protecting him.

56. One would think now these had bid
fair for an absolute breach with *Scotland*,
but they are not satisfy'd yet; one thing
more they will do which they are confident
will do the feat. It is this ; At the coming
in of the *Scots*, they had born them in hand,
they desir'd nothing but the uniting of the
Nations : That therefore they would never
make Peace without their advice and consent ; and that as they desir'd a conjunction
of Forces and Counsels for prosecution of the
War, so whensoever a Peace was made, they
desir'd a conjunction of Counsels and Inte-
rests

*

refts for the prefervation thereof, that fo the Kingdoms, interwoven one with another, might be a mutual ftrength and fecurity one to another. Therefore in framing the pro-pofitions for Peace prefented to the King at *Oxford*, and treated on at *Uxbridg*, which was done at the Committee of the two King-doms, they make it one propofition, That fome Commiffioners from *Scotland* fhould be joined with ours in the power of the Militia of this Kingdom, and converfe fome of ours with theirs in their Kingdom, and fo bring it to the Houfe. Where my felf, and many more, who truly defir'd the joyning of the Nations in love and good underftanding to perpetuity, oppofed it, fearing that joining them in that power would prove a dividing of affection, which fhould be beft fet, and fo preferved by keeping feveral their feveral Interefts. But thofe carry'd it, and what we fear'd prov'd true: it being afterward made an occafion of great endeavours to fet the two Kingdoms farther afunder, and cer-tainly was firft done by them out of that de-fign.

57. For now when the propofitions were to be fent again to the King to *Newcaftle*, that .Party took their rife upon that propofition to have them all review'd, and changed al-moft all in them that look'd towards the *Scots*, and gave themfelves liberty, as they

had

had a large Field, to fhew the inconveniencies of admitting another Kingdom to fhare
power in this. And much was done and
faid reflecting upon *Scotland*, and againft all
fuch intermixtures. Then thofe who fhewed their diflike of it before, and would not
have had it done when it was to do, being
now done, did not defire at that time to have
it undone, in truth, unwilling there fhould
be any altering of the propofitions at all;
not knowing where thefe Men would ftop,
if once they began to change any part : And
therefore offer'd this confideration, that
though before it had been no wrong or un-
kindnefs to our Brethren not to have admitted them to fuch a Copartnerfhip, which
they apprehended would prove rather a prejudice than otherwife, but being now in,
they thought it might be ill taken to thruft
them out, and argue a jealoufie and change
of Affection, according to the Rule, *Tur-
piùs ejicitur quam non admittitur*, &c. But
for that very reafon were thefe Men the
more earneft for it, that it might be ill taken,
that it might argue a jealoufie, that the
Scots might fee by it, that the countenance
of the Parliament was not to them as before, and that the Ligament being untied,.
by which the two Kingdoms did feem to be
bound up together, they might fall in funder, and the breach be the greater. O the
wick-

wickednefs of thefe Men, that thirfted after
nothing but to fee the two Kingdoms wel-
tering in that blood which they muft let out
of one another's Veins! But that does the
more commend the goodnefs, piety, wifdom, and moderation of our Brethren of
Scotland, which prevented it; for notwithftanding all thefe provocations, all thefe injuries and affronts, they were ftedfaft, they
were unmoveable in their refolutions to
promote the Peace of *England*. They faid
they came in to help it, they will not be
made Inftruments to deftroy it : They had
bound themfelves in a Covenant before God,
and in a Treaty with their Brethren of *England*, to endeavour by all good ways and
means a happy Settlement and Reformation
both in Church and State : The art and malice of their Enemies, and the Enemies of
Peace, fhall not engage them to become in
any fort an occafion of hindering it. Therefore they deny themfelves, they renounce
their own intereft, they quit all pretenfions,
and agree with the Parliament in thofe alterations, aand thereby defeat the expectation
of thofe who hop'd to fee, not only the propofitions of Peace laid afide upon that occafion, but that *Scotland* fhould have born the
blame, both of not making Peace with the
King, and alfo of all the Miferies which muft
have followed upon both Kingdoms by a
rupture and breach between 'em. 58.

58. When they saw they could not by
Art and underhand-dealing compass this
Breach, that neither the *Scots* would be pro-
voked to declare against the Parliament, and
so the War begin on that side; nor could
they engage the Northern Counties to fall
upon them : If either of which had taken,
they had still kept themselves behind the
Curtain, and hid the Arm which had thrown
the Stone; they had seem'd, alas, innocent
well-meaning Men, and yet the mischief
befallen which they had contriv'd.   But rather than fail they will throw of the Vizard,
and come downright with open face, to the
executing their Design.   They set on their
Teazers, as *Haslerig, Mildmay, Martin*, and
many others, to move, That Sir *Thomas
Fairfax* might go down with his Army to
protect those Northern Counties, and relieve them from the oppression of the *Scots*,
a pretty way of protection and giving ease,
to send an Army into a Country.   We see
how this Army eases the Country now, to
the breaking both of their backs and hearts.
But, could they have gotten a Vote for this,
their work had been done, and we should
soon have heard of mischief and felt it : The
animosity between those two Armies had
instantly put them and the Kingdoms into
blood, for which, no question, Sir *Thomas
Fairfax* had his Instructions, but the House
would

would never give way to it, tho with earnest-
ness prest many times by that Party. And
when they saw they could not prevail, the
presumptions are very strong, that they would
have had the Army to have march'd thither without the Parliament's order : for the
Scots had an alarm of the Army's moving
towards them, and their Commissioners so
inform'd the House, with a protestation a-
gainst it, upon which there was a stop,
with a denial and disavowment of their having any such intention. Yet certainly there
was an attempt, and it is said, orders out for
part of the Army to move that way ; but God
be thanked it went no further, for that would
have been a sad business.

59. Before I go off this matter, I must do
that right to Col. *Pointz*, who commanded the Northern Forces, as to attribute to
his care and vigilancy, and his discreet or-
dering of his business, a great part of our
happiness, that all that mischief was prevented which was so earnestly endeavour'd
to be pull'd on us, by engaging the Country
and Scotish Army in quarrel and bloodshed;
and that was his Crime with these Men to
be for it, since so unjustly put out of his
Command, after they had stir'd up the unruly Rabble of the Agitators, to take him
by violence out of his House at *York*, being
as absolutely in his Command as *Fairfax* was

in

in his : Meerly doing it by an act of power,
force, and violence, breaking through all
Rules of Juftice, Equity, and Honefty,
bringing him a Prifoner to the Army, not
fuffering him fo much as to put on his
Clothes, or fpeak to his Wife, or any
Friend, but ufe him as if he had been the
greateft Traytor in the world, when Sir
Thomas Fairfax could not pretend to the leaft
jurifdiction over him, nor any thing could
be laid to his charge. Such is their hatred of
every honeft Man, who ftands in their way
to their pernicious defigns.

60. Their next hope was, that the Scotifh Army would not go out of the Kingdom at the defire of the Parliament ; fo bloody Nofes would be upon that occafion : and
I muft give them their due, there was no
failure in them, to do all that was poffible
to have kept them in ftill only to quarrel
with them, but with a feeming to defire
nothing fo much as their going. Very forward they were to get the Vote of the Parliament that they fhould be gone ; but to
inable them to go they would not help, rather hinder, and hang on all the weights
they could. To fay the truth, they had
fome ground to believe, Firft, That they
would not go, Secondly, That they could
not, if they would ; for the *Scots* had a colour, if not juft reafon to have refus'd.

61. By the Covenant and Treaty, the two Kingdoms had bound themselves before God and one to another, as one intire Body, to prosecute the Cause (these are the very words of the Declaration of both Houses to the State of the united Provinces, which Declaration Mr. Sollicitor himself penn'd, therefore they must hold it Canonical) and that neither Kingdom should lay down Arms till the Ends mention'd in the Covenant and Treaty were obtain'd. If then in this Cause the Forces of both Kingdoms made but one intire Body, the *Scots* had a good Plea, Why will you send us away and disband us wholly? This proceeding is not equal, the Body must suffer, and cannot act as an intire Body if one whole Member be cut off; or if there be no more need of acting, if the Ends be obtain'd for which the Body was constituted, and therefore you send us away, then why do you keep up your own Army, the other part of this Body? This had certainly been strong reason, which Mr. Sollicitor would have been puzled to answer.

62. Besides, the *Scots* had cause enough to have their jealousie prompt them, that it was not safe for them to depart with their Army, lay by their Swords, and leave standing in this Kingdom so great a Force, which they knew to be so ill affected to them, and
might

might act to their prejudice ; and the King being in their power, perhaps force both him and the Parliament to a Peace difadvantageous to *Scotland*, and differing from thofe grounds upon which, by the Kingdom of *England*, they were engag'd in this Quarrel : or elfe make no Peace at all, but interpofe (as *Cromwel* to the Earl of *Manchefter*) to hinder it, and themfelves govern by the Sword, not only to the prejudice of *Scotland*, but alfo ruin of *England*. One may fwear there was ground enough for fuch a fear ; for fince it hath prov'd fo to purpofe. But according to the old Rule, they who mean well themfelves, are not fufpicious of others. The *Scots* had no thoughts but of fetling a Peace, laying down of Arms, calling the People, and all things to revert into their old Channel ; therefore they were willing to be gone and return into their own Country, in confidence that after their departure, the Army under Sir *Thomas Fairfax* fhould likewife prefently be disbanded, fince there was no more need of any Army at all, fo they were willing to go.

63. But then the queftion was if they would go or not, and how the Soldiers would be difpos'd to march out, who had not been paid of fo many Months, infomuch as the Scotifh Commiffioners gave in an account of fome 800000 *l.* Arrears. Here our Gallants

lants hop'd they had them upon the Hip,
and fhould furely give them a fall. Then
they thruft on fome of their little Northern
Beagles, as Mr. *Blaxton*, and others, to inform what high Sums they had rais'd upon the Country; upon which they conclude the Scotifh Army was in their debt,
and therefore they would come to an account with them, which had been a fure
way to have kept them in the Kingdom
five or fix months longer. But to help that,
our juft Pay-mafters faid the Army fhould
march away, and fome perfons be left behind to fee all accounts adjufted : which had
requir'd very good Rhetorick to have made
it Juftice, efpecially to have appear'd fo to
the Scotifh Soldiers : for to have fent them
away without Money, and then ask the
Country-man what the Soldiers had taken,
when he might fay what he thought good,
the Soldier not there to anfwer for himfelf,
and yet his Pay to be thereby determin'd,
would have been but hard meafure. But
the Rhetorick had been, Sir *Thomas Fairfax* to have gone down with his Army,
which fhould have made it juft, and eafie,
and every thing; for this was it they defir'd
to bring it to, as it was often mov'd and
prefs'd by them.

64. At laft the well-wifhers to Peace
with much ado prevail'd in the Houfe, and

it was carry'd to offer the *Scots* a grofs Sum
for all, fo to part fair, and avoid the delay
and difputes of an account, to which they
prefently agreed. Then the queftion was
what Sum. Here again we had a ftrong
debate : For our Incendiaries hung by every
twig, fticking faft to their Principles to dif-
fatisfie the *Scots*, and break with them (if
poffible) upon any point ; pretending the
poverty of the Kingdom, and the great Sums
the *Scots* had rais'd, and therefore they
would give but 100000 *l.* which they knew
was all one with a hundred Shillings, as to
the fatisfying of the Soldiers for marching
away. In the end, after many debates in
the Houfe, and paffages to and again with
the Scotch Commiffioners, the loweft Sum
that could be agreed unto by the Commiffioners was 400000 *l.* two in hand, and the
other two after fome time, with a proteftation of theirs, that the Army would
not be fatisfy'd with lefs, nor inabled to
march, which was motive enough for thefe
Men to deny it ; for if they could have
wrought the diffatisfaction of the Army,
fo as to have refus'd to go, it was where
they would have it. Whereupon 'twas oppos'd by them with all the power they had,
but in the end the better part, that is the moderate Party, who were the Peace-makers,
thofe that labour'd to keep things even and
                                            fair

fair between the two Kingdoms, carry'd it:
And the fum was voted, and all things
agreed upon, tho with difficulty (for
they fought it out and loft it by Inches)
then the *Scots* declar'd they would march out
by fuch a day.

65. Yet had our *Boutefeu* one hope left,
which was to quarrel at laft about the perfon of the King, believing the *Scots* would
certainly have taken his Majefty with them
into *Scotland*. This they knew had been
ground fufficient, and would have engag'd
all *England* againft them, giving a confirma-
tion to all the jealoufies formerly rais'd, and
occafion'd a thoufand more: And had certainly more advantag'd the defigns of thofe
who thirfted after the deftruction of the
King firft, the *Scots* next, and then all fuch
as defir'd Peace within this Kingdom, and
have made them a fmoother way to their
damnable Ends, the altering of the Government, and bringing in a confufion both in
Church and State, than any thing that could
have happen'd: And the two Kingdoms
had been together in blood, the author of the
mifchief undifcover'd, mask'd over with the
glorious pretences of zealoufly vindicating
the honefty and intereft of *England*, and e-
very breach of Coven... ...nd Treaty in this
Caufe, which mad... ...with fo much pe-
remptorinefs a... ...and in truth i...

justice, demand that the *Scots* would deliver up his Majesty, who had an equal interest in his Royal Person with the Kindom of
England, he being equally King of both,
and an equal interest in the closing and binding up the unhappy differences which were
between him and both his Kingdoms, they
having been engag'd in that Quarrel at
the entreaty of *England*, and made up together with an intire Body with *England*
(as is before shewed) for the prosecution
of it. Therefore they had no more reason
to trust us with the King than we had
them; and as much were they concern'd
in all that related to his Majesty's Person,
so as they had ground enough to have dif-
puted it, and out of that hope was it press'd
by the others. But the wisdom of the Scotish Nation foresaw the inconveniencies
which must have necessarily follow'd, had
they been positive at that time, how they had
plaid their Enemies game to their own ruin, and even ruin to his Majesty. Therefore
they made for him the best conditions they
could, that is for the safety and honour of
his Person, and to avoid greater mischiefs,
were necessitated to leave him in *England*,
and so march away. Which they did in
February 1646.

66. Here then the very mouth of Ini-
quity was stopt, Malice it self had nothing
to

to fay to give the leaft blemifh to the faithfulnefs and reality of the Kingdom of *Scotland*, the clearnefs of their Proceedings, their zeal for Peace, without felf-feeking and felf-ends, to make advantage of the miferies and misfortunes of *England*. This gave fuch a reputation to them, and to thofe that appear'd for them (that is, fo far for them, as to endeavour the doing of them right, and prevent the practices of thofe who fought all means of doing them wrong) and gave fuch a blow to the other violent Party, fo broke their power, and leffen'd their authority in the Parliament, as it made way for obtaining thofe refolutions which were prefently taken for disbanding Sir *Thomas Fairfax*'s Army. Till when, by the fomenting jealoufies againft the *Scots*, and againft all moderate and well affected perfons, as if their defigns were to betray the Caufe, deliver over the Honour, and Intereft, and Strength of *England*, into the hands of the *Scots*, they prevail'd fo far, generally upon the affection of the people, and efpecially upon many well-meaning (but not fo well difcerning) perfons, Members of Parliament, as they were able to fupprefs all good motions tending towards Peace, all endeavours of fmoothing thofe rugged ways that their violence had put all things in, and to fwell up that Independent Army, like the

F 3 Spleen

Spleen in the Body by the concourse of all ill
humours, to the ruin and confumption of
the Body it felf: And yet other Forces ca-
fhier'd, as Major General *Maffey*'s Brigade,
which had done all the Service in the Weft,
of which thofe Drones robb'd the fweet, getting the honour and advantage of it to themfelves. That tho that Army was compos'd for the moft part of factious Sectaries,
except fome few gallant Men that were fcat-
ter'd here and there amongft them, as Colonel *Greves*, Colonel *Thomas Sheffield*, Sir
Robert Pye, Colonel *Herbert*, Colonel *But-
ler*, Quarter-Mafter General *Finober*, and
other Officers of Quality, and Gentlemen of
the Life-Guard, who had formerly ferv'd
under my Lord of *Effex*, and Sir *William
Waller*, and in other parts of the Kingdom,
to whom they did the honour of letting them
perform all the Action which that Army
had to do, and who every one of them afterward left it, when it left its obedience to
the Parliament and fidelity to the Kingdom, and that they grew to be not only an
unneceffary grievous burden in refpect of
charge, but alfo a let and hinderance to the
fetling all Government both civil and eccle-
fiaftical, neither fubmitting themfelves to
order of Parliament, nor permitting others
where they could hinder it; but giving
countenance to all diforders, efpecially in
the

the Church, as breaking open the Church doors, doing moft unfeemly barbarous things, indeed not fit to be related either to modeft or Chriftian Ears, and in time of Divine Service interrupting Minifters as they were preaching, mifcalling, reviling them, fometimes pulling them down by violence, beating and abufing them, getting into the Pulpits themfelves, and venting either ridiculous or fcandalous things, falfe and pernicious Doctrins, countenancing and publifhing feditious Pamphlets (for which they had a Prefs that follow'd the Army) decrying both King and Parliament and all Authority, infufing a rebellious Spirit into the people, under the pretence of Liberty and Freedom. All this notwithftanding while the Scotifh Army was in the Kingdom. Such things were whifper'd, fuch jealoufies and fears rais'd, as thefe inconveniencies were not only difpens'd with, but the Army fupported and cherifh'd as if they had been tutelary Gods, thofe who muft have protected and deliver'd us from all danger, and all that the Parliament and Kingdom could do, little enough to feed and maintain them, tho an excrefcence that drew away the whole nourifhment of the Body, and ftarv'd it.

67. But afterwards when the Kingdom faw how they had been abus'd, made to fear

where

where no fear was, and were come to themselves, they soon grew to feel the weight of that which lay upon them, and seek for ease. Then City and Country could petition the Parliament for disbanding the Army, complain of their intolerable disorders and irregularities, and the Parliament was well dispos'd for it, who now likewise discover'd the art and malice of the Independent Party, a Spirit they had rais'd which they would gladly lay, and consider'd, that as such an Army was dangerous, so none at all was needful, that *Ireland* wanted what we had too much of, Soldiers.

68. Besides, they well saw that whilst that Army stood, they should never be able to relieve *Ireland* to any purpose, the stock of the Kingdom was swallow'd up in their maintenance; and tho for the space of a whole year there had not been an Enemy in the Field, nor Town possess'd by any to find them employment, yet they recruited daily, all care being taken for sending them Pay, Arms, Provision, Clothes, with all other necessaries, as if they were every day upon hard and dangerous Service, when they did nothing but trouble and oppress the Country; so as notwithstanding their glorious pretences of fighting for Conscience, not Pay, sacrificing themselves to God and the Kingdom's Cause, none of them would stir to

to help the poor Proteſtants in that King-dom, but even hinder'd what they could all others from going.

69. Which appear'd by Colonel ~~Ham-mond~~'s Capitulation, being deſign'd for the Service of *Dublin*, who tho he were but an Enſign to Sir *Simon Harcourt* in the begin-ing of thoſe Wars, now a Colonel of the new Model, ſtood upon his pantoufles, That he would not be oblig'd for longer than two or three Months, have all his Pay be-fore hand, Victuals for ſix Months tho he would ſtay but two, be abſolute Command-er of all the Forces there, have a proportion of Money over and above for contingent occaſions put into what hands he would appoint, a Fleet of Ships to tranſport him, wait upon him, and be at his diſpoſing, not to ſtir without his leave; in truth he muſt be Admiral and General; ſuch Terms as no Prince or foreign State that had but given an aſſiſtance could have ſtood upon higher. This was the obedient conſcientious Army; but moſt Men were ſatisfy'd if it was not disbanded *Ireland* muſt be loſt, and *England* undone.

70. The Parliament therefore taking in-to their conſideration the neceſſity of relie-ving that dying Kingdom, after long debate, and much oppoſition from all that Party, came at laſt to a reſolution in *May* 1647,

and

and vote, that a certain proportion of Foot and Horse should forthwith be transported into *Ireland* (as I remember seven Regiments of Foot, of which four I am certain were to be taken out of the Army) they further vote, that no Foot should be continu'd in *England*, but those that were to be for the necessary defence of the Garisons, and that about five thousand Horse and Dragoons should remain under Pay in this Kingdom, for quieting and preventing any stir or trouble, either within or from abroad, to interrupt proceedings till a settlement of Affairs: Peoples Minds after such Commotions being, like the Sea after a Storm, unquiet for some time tho the wind be abated. Those Men would have had a far greater number, and press'd it earnestly, saying, We laid by our strength that all might be deliver'd back into the King's hands; and tho even this proportion seem'd very great to discreet and moderate Men, yet they pitch'd upon it, partly to stop the mouths of these Railers, and give satisfaction to all indifferent persons, who look'd not so far into business, and were apt enough to be misled into jealousies and suspicions, and partly because they well hop'd it would be but for some short time that this charge should be continu'd upon the Kingdom.

7ɪ.

71. Here then is the Ax first laid to the root of this broad spreading Tree, the Army; a dismal Cypress, the shadow and dropping whereof were so pernicious as to darken all the comfortable beams of our Sun-shine of Peace, and suffer no good thing to prosper near it; this vext the Children of darkness, who now must cast about, shake Heaven and Earth, raise all the black Spirits of Hell, confound Sea and Land, and all the Elements, rather than permit this to take place.

72. The Parliament goes on with this work, refers it to the Committee of Lords and Commons at *Derby-house*, to see those Votes concerning *Ireland* put in execution. The eleven Members were almost all of them of that Committee, who may say *Hinc illæ Lacrimæ.* For doing their parts, together with the rest, in discharge of the duty and trust which lay upon them to take care of that poor Kingdom, and discovering the designs of the Army to frustrate all the good designs of the Parliament, they incur the mortal hatred of the Party and Army which have driven them from their Homes, and Country, and City of *London*, without the privity or consent of the House of Parliament. The Earl of *Warwick*, the Lord *Dacres*, Sir *William Waller*, Sir *John Clotworthy*, Major General *Massey*, and Mr. *Salloway*,

loway, are the perſons employ'd. Theſe labour to diſpoſe Officers and Soldiers to a compliance with the neceſſities of *Ireland*; but at the very firſt were receiv'd with a mutinous acclamation amongſt the Officers whom they had call'd together, ſome of them crying out, One and all, and the whole Company diſturb'd and diſtemper'd. So as finding it not convenient to deal with them together in a body, they deſir'd, that ſuch as had a ſenſe of the miſerable condition of that Kingdom, and a will to ingage for the relief of it, would repair to them to their Lodgings, which very many did, Colonels and Lieutenant Colonels, and other Officers, and undertook for themſelves, and a very conſiderable number of their Soldiers, about 1500, or 2000, caſting themſelves wholly upon the Parliament for their conditions. The reſt of the Officers and Soldiers of the Army doing all that was poſſible to obſtruct the Service, decrying the Employment, railing upon, miſuſing, threatning, and thereby diſcourage thoſe who engag'd, calling them deſerters of the Army and of their General, and by great offers and aſſurance of better conditions to ſtay with them keeping of others.

73. And at that very time did ſome of the Officers meet and prepare a Petition, together with a Repreſentation, in the name

of

of the whole Army, That before disbanding
there might be an Act of Indemnity with
the King's royal Assent to it ; that Auditors
might speedily repair to the Army to cast
up their Accounts for their Service from the
beginning ; that none who had serv'd volun-
tarily in that Army should be compel'd to
go out of the Kingdom ; th●●ill disbanded,
Money might be sent down for their supply.
This was a fair beginning of the godly Army's taking care for *Ireland*, and of those
good Officers proceedings, so obedient to
the Parliament, as meerly for that they had
been made choice of and put into the rooms
of far better Men than themselves ; now forsooth, when the Parliament would have some
of them go for *Ireland*, they will put the
whole Army into a Mutiny.

74. For an Army, or any part of it, to
join in a Petition, tho but for Pay, when
their Superiors (that Authority which they
are to obey) require any Duty to be perform'd, or Service to be done by them, as
the present relieving of *Ireland* was, this,
I think, by the Rules of War, has in all
Armies been held a Mutiny, and the Authors, at least, punish'd with death. Here
to be sure it shall mutiny to purpose, and
not disband according to the resolutions of
Parliament ; they put them not only to petition in this mutinous way, but to desire
im-

impoſſibilities, as *Tacitus* ſays, *Non ut aſſe-querentur ſed tauſam ſeditioni,* not to reſt ſa-tisfy'd with former Ordinances, and the ge-neral care taken for all who had ſerv'd in theſe unhappy Wars, but to demand a par-ticular Act of Indemnity with his Maje-ſty's approbation, not that they car'd for him, or meant ever to ſee him again in power to enact any thing, which their pro-ceedings ſince have made clear to all mens underſtandings (though ſome diſcern'd it very well to be their principle and their drift from the beginning) but they knew this would take up time, could not poſſibly be ſo ſoon done, and would elude all endea-vours of disbanding. So for Auditors to go and caſt up their Accounts was the work of many Months, and a ſtrange demand for this godly obedient Army to make, who, by their own ſayings, were not Mercenary, but had taken up Arms in judgment and conſcience, and out of love and duty to the Parliament, not for their Pay. Their other demand is as good, and is as much as to ſay, as that the Parliament ſhould ſend none of them for *Ireland,* they who were the Parlia-ments Army, who, as Mr. *Cromwel* made us believe, would go with a word to any part of the World, whither the Parliament would pleaſe to ſend them ; and therefore the other Armies and Major General *Maſſey's* Forces muſt

must be cashier'd (those who certainly would have gone) to make way for their entertainment. These now who had receiv'd the Pay of the Kingdom so long, the sole Army, which, like *Pharaoh*'s lean Kine, had eaten all the rest, and had the Sword of the Parliament singly, and wholly, in their hands, stand upon terms, and will not be compell'd to go, that is, will not go; for they know none is compell'd for *Ireland*, nor was there any thought of it, since many were willing to ingage in that War, who were not so in this; but this was enough to possess the Army with a prejudice against the imployment, and against the intentions and proceedings of Parliament.

75. This Petition and other of their practices so interrupted the business, that our Commissioners at their return inform'd both Houses of it, who yet were so tender of conceiving or expressing any great dislike of the contrivers and promoters of the Petition for obstructing the Service of *Ireland*, and distempering the Army, and that those who had but been drawn in it should not find themselves lessen'd in their good Opinion, who resolv'd to pass by all, and punish none, except such as should mutinously persist in the promoting of it. They sent likewise up for some of the Officers that had more notoriously appear'd therein, and in discouraging

raging and abusing them who offer'd themselves in the Irish Service : Whose miscarriage, though it was very gross, and the answers of some of them at the House of Commons Bar mere collusion and equivocation (as by name Lieutenant Colonel *Pride*'s, who being charg'd with causing the Petition to be read at the head of his Regiment, deny'd it stoutly, because, it seems, it was but at the head of every Company, the Regiment not being drawn up together) notwithstanding all this, the House willing to bury what was past, and hoping it would have gain'd them to a better obedience for the future, sent them down again, rather with respect than otherwise, acquiescing with their denyal. And this very act of Clemency was turn'd against them ; and afterwards when the Army came to do their work barefac'd, no longer to excuse but justifie that Petition, nay, make the Parliament criminous for questioning it, they upbraided the House with sending up for the Officers from their Charge, when they had nothing to say to them.

76. The necessity of disbanding more and more appearing, it hastens the resolutions for it ; whereupon it was order'd, that Officers and Soldiers should have six weeks Pay of their Arrears, and so be disbanded, those

thofe that would be taken in for *Ireland* to have fix weeks more advance. The Parliament at firft pitch'd upon no greater Sum, it being the higheft that had yet been given to any. Major General *Maffey*'s Brigade, which had been much longer without Pay, and had done better Service, had no more. The other Armies under my Lord of *Effex,* and Sir *William Waller*, which had likewife done more work, the chief and main of it all, as having had a ftronger Force to grapple with, and yet had receiv'd lefs Wages, were put off with a fortnights Pay. This made the Parliament think this proportion fufficient; yet afterwards they of themfelves increas'd it to two months, which was more than any had before. Suppofing then there would be no queftion of a compliance, they proceed to perfect what was further neceffary for the fupply of *Ireland,* and fafety of *England.*

77. For *England* they appointed what Regiments of Horfe and Dragoons fhall ftand, fettle the Garifons, name Sir *Thomas Fairfax* General of all the Forces under Pay, which was fufficient Honour for him for the Service he had done; and fhew'd that they had no meaning to difmifs thofe with reproach who had ferv'd them, as they were falfely fcandaliz'd.

G

78.

78. For *Ireland*, they make Serjeant Major General *Skippon* Commander in Chief, with the Title of Field Marſhal, and Major General *Maſſey* Lieutenant General of the Horſe; recommended it to the care of the Committee at *Derby-houſe*, to prepare all things neceſſary for the forwarding of that Service, and draw off ſuch of the Army as were willing to go : for the diſtempers there continu'd, thoſe who had declar'd themſelves being affronted, diſcourag'd, and many of them debaucht from that Service.

79. This was faithfully perform'd by the Committee (that is, by part of it) for ſome of them, as the Sollicitor, *Cromwel*, Sir *Arthur Haſlerig*, and thoſe of that gang would not attend, but the others did. And if I may ſpeak it without vanity, it being one of the great Crimes with which the eleven Members ſtand charg'd, by their care and induſtry, they put the whole buſineſs into ſuch a way, not only doing their beſt endeavours to have ſent over the Forces that ſhould have gone out of the Army, but ſending over others alſo, as Colonel *Jones*, and thoſe Regiments which went to *Dublin*, and ſupplying the beſt they could my Lord *Inchiqueen*, and thoſe Forces which were there before, with ſuch neceſſaries as they could provide, that by the bleſſing of God the foundation was laid for all the good which has ſince

be-

befallen that Kingdom, and for the great advantages which thofe gallant Men have gotten upon the Rebels, notwithftanding the little affiftance they have fince receiv'd, having, in truth, been rather hinder'd than helpt; for every body knows the malice which is born them by that Party which now bears fway, what difcouragements my Lord *Inchiqueen* has labour'd under, and the fmall regard had of Colonel *Jones.* Yet they have fubfifted, and not only preferv'd but advanc'd very much the Englifh Intereft, with Honour to themfelves, and fhame to thefe unworthy Men who are fo little fenfible of the conditions of the poor Proteftants there, preferring their particular revenge and profecution of their damnable End before all that is of Honour and Juftice, and either of duty to God and their Country, or compaffion to their diftreffed Brethren.

80. The Officers in the mean time play their parts below in the Army, they had already engag'd the Soldiers to ftand upon Pay, an Act of Indemnity, and fome other Immunities, plaufible things to make them all of a piece, enter into a kind of a league and combination one with another, and fo become fit to receive any other impreffion, and unite upon it. Therefore now they go a ftep further, to incenfe them againft the

Par-

Parliament, mifreprefenting all paffages and proceedings to them, as if the intention were to force them for *Ireland,* and therefore ftarve them or difmifs them with fhame, and expofe them to queftion and trouble for what they had done in the Wars ; fo engaging them to perfift upon their demands in that Petition, and ask reparation of the Parliament for wrong done them by the Commiffioners fent down for the bufinefs of *Ireland,* and other Members of the Houfe, whom they had characteriz'd to be Enemies to the Army, whereby they put them into fuch a diftemper, as all thoughts of duty and obedience were caft off, nothing fo odious as the Parliament, nothing would fatisfie but revenge.

81. When they had wrought the Feat, Sir *Thomas Fairfax* himfelf came to *London* upon pretence of taking Phyfick ; *Cromwel, Ireton, Fleetwood, Rainsborough,* who were Members of the Houfe of Commons as well as principal Officers of the Army, keep the Houfe, that the Soldiers might be left to themfelves to fire the more, run up to extremes, and put themfelves into a pofture to carry on their work of Rebellion with a high and violent hand, which had been fo handfomly done : for either they muft have appear'd in it and join'd with the Soldiers, which had been too grofs, or have ftop'd it

in

in the beginning, crufh'd the Serpent in the Egg, which had been moft eafie, but was contrary to their defign. So now they give the bufinefs time to foment, and the Rebellion to grow to fome head, that afterwards when they fhould come amongft them (for they could not but expect the Parliament would fend them down) they might feem to be carry'd with the violence, and to give fome way for preventing greater inconveniences, and to keep them from extremities till the Monfter was form'd, and got to that ftrength as to protect it felf and them, when they might without danger declare for it, which they afterwards did. In the mean time difclaiming it, blaming the Soldiers at that diftance (as *Cromwel* did openly in the Houfe, protefting, for his part, he would ftick to the Parliament) whilft underhand they fent them encouragements and directions; for nothing was done there, but by advice and countenance from *London*, where the whole bufinefs was fo laid, the Rebellion refolv'd upon, and the Officers that were in town fo deeply engag'd, that when the full time was come for putting things in execution, my friend *Cromwel*, who had been fent down by the Parliament to do good Offices, was come up again without doing any, and he who had made thofe folemn publick Proteftations with fome great Imprecations on himſelf if he fail'd in his performance, did, notwithſtanding, privily convey thence his Goods (which many of the Independents likewiſe did, leaving City and Parliament as mark'd out for deſtruction) and then without leave of the Houſe (after ſome Members miſſing him and fearing him gone, had mov'd to have him ſent for; whereupon he being, as it ſeems, not yet gone, and having notice of it, came and ſhew'd himſelf a little in the Houſe) did ſteal away that evening, I may ſay run away poſt down to the Army, and preſently join in the Subſcription of a rebellious Letter, whereof I ſhall ſpeak anon. But let him take heed thoſe Imprecations fall not upon him, which many times God remembers, and takes Men at their word, meeting with them in their diſſembling wiſhes, when themſelves leaſt think of them, perhaps have forgot that ever they made them. This by the way.

82. For the preſent the thing pitch'd upon was to ſet up a kind of Council (like the ſupreme Council of the Iriſh Rebels, but that thoſe were moſt of them perſons of birth and degree, theſe *ex face populi*) under the name of Agitators. Two (as I take it) were choſen out of every Regiment, at firſt, I think, but common Soldiers (tho afterwards ſome Officers were ad-

added) to transact this business. These now, forsooth, seem to acknowledg no Officer, but to rule and dispose of all things as they think good. They take into consideration what is fit to be done, what not, and give their orders accordingly, examine and censure the Orders and Votes of Parliament, receive all Complaints, give the redress, send out their Warrants and Commands, write their Letters, exercise a general power over all, set up a new form of Government in the Army, and in the end are instrumental to their Masters to possess themselves of his Majesty's Person, subdue Parliament, City, and Kingdom, and be reveng'd upon all those who had formerly given any disturbance to the carrying on of their design, till such time as the work was done which they had set them to do. But then Mr. *Cromwel* and his Officers could give a stop to their proceedings. And when the Agitators thought to do as formerly, and finish'd what they were made to believe should be the Catastrophe of their Tragedy, which was the destruction of the King, and alteration of the Government, Counsels not being at that time so dispos'd, nor the time ripe for the execution, they soon found their Locks were cut, and (the influence of their Superiors ceasing) their strength fail'd, so as they brought but confusion to them-

selves;

selves; three of the chief were condemn'd to die for mutiny, but *Cromwel* being a merciful Prince would take but one, who was shot to death, the rest reduced to subjection and obedience, their Council Table dissolv'd, and their Castles in the Air vanish'd to smoak. But these things fell out long after, for a time they triumph, act all, drive on the design ; *Cromwel* and his fellows standing behind the Curtain, laught in their sleeves, and pleas'd themselves to see the Game which they had packt, play so well.

83. The first Act of these new Rulers, was a Letter sent to their three principal Officers, who were then in *London*, and innocent persons, God knows, knew nothing of all this, Sir *Thomas Fairfax*, Lieutenant General *Cromwel*, and Serjeant Major General *Skippon*. For this last, to do him right, I think that at that time he was innocent indeed ; but afterwards I must avow it, he, together with the help of Mr. *Marshal* a Minister, contributed more, to the success of their Villanies, betraying the Parliament and City into their hands, than all that *Cromwel*, the Sollicitor, *Ireton*, and the rest of the Crew did or could do, and no question will be sufficiently rewarded for it by them ; for they are good at it to pay dear out of the publick Store for any man's Conscience that will be sold, and may be useful to them.

84.

*

84. This Letter was an exclamation against the Parliament, falfe and untrue Complaints of wrongs done to the Soldiers at Affizes in the Counties, a proteftation againft the Irifh Expedition, calling it a defign to break the Army, declaring if any of thefe three Commanders fhould engage, their averfenefs to it (tho one of them, *Skippon*, was by the Parliament appointed, and had accepted it) in plain Englifh faying they would not disband, nor receive any other propofitions from the Parliament till their expectations were fatisfy'd. Three of the Agitators brought it, and *Skippon* acquainted the Houfe with it; they were fent for, and carry'd themfelves at the Bar in a flighting braving manner, refufing to anfwer fuch queftions as the Speaker, by order of the Houfe, ask'd them; faying they were employ'd by the Army, and could not without leave from thence difcover any thing. Many the Houfe refenting this high affront, were earneft to have them feverely punifh'd; but that Party ftood as ftifly for them, infomuch that the worthy Burgefs of *Newcaftle*, Mr. *Warmworth*, ftood up and faid he would have them committed indeed, but it fhould be to the beft Inn of the Town, and good Sack and Sugar provided them, which was as ridiculous, as 'twas a bold and infolent fcorn put upon the Parliament; at laft even

Mr.

Mr. *Skippon* himself excused them, said they were honest Men, and wisht they might not be too severely dealt with: whereupon the House flatted, let them go without punishment, and by tameness encreas'd their madness and presumption. Whereas had they serv'd them as Mr. *Cromwel* afterwards did their fellows, hang'd one of them (they all well deserving it) it might probably have given a stop to their Career, and prevented a great deal of mischief, which has since befallen the Kingdom by their means.

85. All that we did (whether it was Fate or Design I know not, but it prov'd our Ruin) was to command down to the Army the Officers that were Members of the House, such as were in town, and the General himself. I say, I know not if there were a design in it; because afterwards upon just such another occasion, we sent Sir *Henry Vane* the younger, Mr. *Scawen*, and some others, which I am sure was a thing laid; and this wrought the same effect as that did, even put them together the better to contrive and lay their business, joining the counsels of the Officers to the actings of the Agitators, so to hatch that horrid Rebellion which soon after broke out, to the utter ruin (if God's hand of mercy interpose not) of Parliament and Kingdom. They were sent to allay the distempers, and to prevent in-

inconveniencies, but how they difcharg'd that truft will foon appear.

86. Inftead of difcountenancing, repro-ving, and fuppreffing that difpofition to mu-tiny, that ftanding upon terms with the Parliament, thofe Meetings and Confultati-ons by which the ill humour was nourifh'd, and inftead of perfwading them to a fitting obedience and fubmiffion, and laying the Regiments farther afunder to leffen and a-bate the contagion, they gave them occafion to encreafe their diftempers and vent them, by asking them what they will have, calling the Officers together, and fending them to their feveral Regiments to be inform'd of their defigns; and by drawing them together already fo indifpos'd and inflam'd, inflame them the more. A ftrange way of quieting an Army that was in a way to Rebellion, and had begun to fet up a new Government amongft themfelves by their Agitators, which fped accordingly, and produced the effect that they defir'd, a reprefentation of Grievances, in which the whole Army now join'd and engag'd, except fome few gallant Men, both Officers and Soldiers, who de-tefted thofe proceedings.

87. This Reprefentation is brought up to the Houfe by Lieutenant General *Cromwel*, and Colonel *Fleetwood*, who had the faces to fay (juft as the Reprefentation begins) That

the

the Army was quiet and free from any vifible diftemper, 'which was only to amufe us. But then it expoftulates with the Parliament the making of the foremention'd Declaration, fending for up and queftioning thofe perfons who had been complain'd of for obftructing the Service of *Ireland*, juftifies them, taxes the Commiffioners of Parliament, and other Members of the Houfe, for doing ill offices to the Army, ftands upon all the particulars of the firft Petition.

88. The Houfe was very much diffatisfy'd with thefe proceedings, and if ever it deny'd it felf, did it then : for it was willing to give the Army fatisfaction in all things poffible, to free the Kingdom of that burden, even difpenfing with their own Honours.

89. They pafs feveral Ordinances for Indemnity, freeing from preffing the relief of maim'd Soldiers, Widows, and Orphans, with fuch alterations and amendments as the Army defir'd. Concerning the propofition of Pay upon disbanding, which was eight weeks, they conceiv'd it could not be inlarg'd, in regard of the great prefent expence to which they were neceffitated for the fupply of *Ireland*;.That the two hundred thoufand Pounds, which for thofe two occafions were then borrow'd of the City of *London*, would fcarce ferve.

90.

90. Therefore upon thefe terms both Houfes concluded the disbanding, begin with the Foot, and appoint to every Regiment, as they lay quarter'd, a Rendevous at fome Town near, where they were to lay down their Arms, receive their Money, and have Paffes to their feveral homes. Thofe that would engage for *Ireland* to march to fome other place near hand, there to receive Advance-money and further Orders.

91. The feveral Ordinances and Orders were fent to Sir *Thomas Fairfax*, who then had his head quarters at *Bury*; and two Lords and four Commoners were appointed Commiffioners to repair to the feveral places appointed for disbanding, with Money, and directions to fee the Service perform'd, and affift Sir *Thomas Fairfax* in it, who was defir'd to iffue out his Orders for the Regiments drawing to thofe places.

92. Then it was refer'd to a Committee of the Army to put into a way, the ftating of the Accounts, both of Officers and Soldiers; and where more than two Months appear'd to be due, the Commiffion Officer was to receive his Debenter from the Committee and Treafurer of the Army, it being appointed where he fhould be paid. The inferior Officer and common Soldier was to have his fecurity upon the Excife.

cise. Let any Man now judg if the Army
had any cause to complain, if all was not
done that with any colour of reason and modesty could be expected.

93. Our Commissioners, who were the
Earl of *Warwick*, the Lord *De la Ware*, Sir
Gilbert Gerard, Mr. *Grinston*, and two o-
thers, went to *Chelmsford* the first of *June*,
the Rendevous appointed for the General's
Regiment, whither the Lieutenant Colonel
came, Lieutenant Colonel *Jackson*, an honest and gallant Man, with a resolution to
conform to the Order of Parliament; but a
Command comes from the General to the
Regiment to march another way for drawing the Quarter near together.

94. For upon the 29th of *May*, when the
Votes were sending down for disbanding,
Sir *Thomas Fairfax* had call'd a Council of
War of the factious Officers (the honest Officers who were for submitting to the Parliament, and a quiet disbanding, having before been most of them abus'd, and forc'd a-
way by the violence of the Soldiers and
commands of the Agitators, he conniving at
it) where they resolve upon an humble Advice to his Excellency, That since their
Grievances were not at all satisfy'd, and
Jealousies were very great, it would not be
safe to disband, but rather draw the Army
into a close posture (there being a great
pro-

propenfity in the Soldiers to a general Rendevous) and then refume the confideration
of their Grievances, and of the Votes for
disbanding, fufpending, for the prefent a-
ny proceedings upon thefe Votes; which
advice his Excellency follows.   So the Parliament commands to disband, Sir *Thomas*
to march away, and draw to a Rendevous:
Fit he fhould be obey'd.

95. At the very fame time Colonel *Rainf-
borough* dos the like with his Regiment
which was at *Petersfield* in *Hampfhire*, defign'd for *Jerfey*, and fo far upon the way,
himfelf being attending the Houfe of Commons, of which he was a Member, and
pretending to prepare for that Employment
which had been entrufted to him; but in
truth to give his Soldiers opportunity to
mutiny, as the reft of the Army did; who,
to give them more time for it, would not
prefently acquaint the Houfe with the Intelligence he had receiv'd of their diforder,
but having it in the morning kept it to himfelf till towards the evening, even denying
his knowledg of any fuch thing, when Sir
William Lewis inform'd the Houfe of it, and
about five or fix a Clock in the Afternoon
(the Houfe then by accident fitting, as thefe
deportments of the Army gave them caufe
fufficient) fpoke of it, faid they were in a
great diftemper, refolv'd not to march to
the

the Sea fide, but return to *Oxford*; whereupon being fent down to quiet them, and
réduce them to obedience, he went immediately, but put himfelf at the head of them,
and inftead of taking care for *Jerfey*,
march'd to *Oxford* firft, fo to the Army ;
and none more violent in the Rebellion than
he : for which good Service, and joyning
with the Agitators in their higheft exorbi-
tancies for the deftruction of the King and
altering of Government, and particularly in
a Petition for taking away the Houfe of
Lords, the Houfe of Commons fince made
him Vice Admiral. And the Lords, to the
eternizing the honour for their gentle tame
difpofitions, confented.

96. But one thing was yet wanting (as
they thought) for the carrying on their defign, and amufing the poor people of *England* with an expectation of their fettling a
Peace, fo to make them fit ftill and look on,
whilft they trampled upon Parliament, City
and Kingdom, which was to be poffeft of the
King's Perfon, and make the world believe
they would bring him up to his Parliament,
and fet him on his Throne. For this it
feems a meeting was appointed at Lieutenant General *Cromwel's*, upon the thirtieth
of *May*, where it is refolv'd, That Cornet
Joyce fhould, with a Party of Horfe, go to
Holmby and feize upon his Majefty, which
is

is prefently executed, and given out, that
others had the like defign, which they had
prevented. At firft it muft feem only to be
the act of Mr. *Joyce*, *Cromwel* protefted he
knew nothing of it (tho he was the Man
appointed it to be done, as appears by what
has been recited, taken out of fome of their
own Authors, one that calls himfelf *Sirrah
Niho*, and others) Sir *Thomas Fairfax* writes
a Letter to the Houfe, profeffes the fame for
himfelf as in the prefence of God, with a
large undertaking for the reft of his Officers,
and the body of the Army. And perhaps he
faid true, I would fain be fo charitable as to
believe it ; nor indeed do I think the good
Man is privy to all their Plots, he muft
have no more than what they are pleas'd to
carve and chew for him, but muft fwallow
all, and own them when they come abroad.
Here then they have the King, *Joyce* drives
away the Guards, forc'd Colonel *Greaves* to
fly, whom elfe they threaten'd to kill, for
no man's life muft ftand in their way (Murder being no Sin in the vifible Saints) carries away his Majefty and the Commiffioners
that attend him Prifoners, and immediately
fends up a Letter to certifie what he had
done, with directions it fhould be deliver'd
to *Cromwel*, and he abfent, to Sir *Arthur
Haflerig*, or Colonel *Fleetwood*, which was
given to Colonel *Fleetwood*, as one Lieute-

H   nant

nant *Markham* inform'd the House, saying, the Messenger that brought it told him so: nor did Sir *Arthur Haslerig* make a clear answer when he was ask'd concerning it in the House, Colonel *Fleetwood* being at that time gone to the Army, so as he could not be examin'd.

97. By this trick they hope to catch the people, and so find no resistance to their traiterous proceedings; yet they will not trust only to Jugling, they will play a sure Game, and have power in their hands to go through the work, and make their way if it will not be given. Therefore the Army must be put into a posture for it, they have the Soldiers already, they must have Artillery and Ammunition; so at the same meeting *Cromwel* likewise appoints *Joyce* (as the same Authors relate) to repair to *Oxford*, secure that Garison, the Magazine and Train of Artillery which had there lain many Months, the Army having had nothing to do, and so no use for it, which therefore the Parliament had then order'd to be remov'd and brought back to the Tower, the place where all Stores are kept. But those who were sent down by the Parliament for that purpose, were by these Mutineers beaten and wounded, the Magazine and Train kept away by force, and besides, some 3 or 4000 *l.* in Money taken from them,

them, which they had carry'd down for dif-
banding of the Regiment there in Garifon.
And now they think they have all in their
own hands, the Fifh is catcht, they may
throw away the Net. They begin there-
forre to appear in their own Colours; *Cromwel*, *Ireton*, with the reft of the Cabal, and
Sir *Thomas Fairfax* in the laft place (who,
tho he be General, is not to lead, but will
be fure to follow clofe) may not lay afide
their innocency and their ignorance (for
all this while they knew nothing) and put
themfelves in the head of the Agitators, own
all they have done, and at *Triploe* Heath,
near *Cambridg*, appoint a general Rendevous, there to declare themfelves, and a-
vowedly enter into the Confederacy.

96. At this Rendevous was fram'd that
folemn Engagement, wherein, they fay,
they look upon the refolutions of the Parliament for their disbanding, as proceeding
from malicious and mifchievous Principles
and Intentions, and not without carnal and
bloody purpofes. That therefore they are
refolv'd not to appear at the places thereto
appointed, and then declare, agree, and pro-
mife to and with each other, That till they
have fuch fatisfaction in all their Grievances,
and fuch fecurity for the future as fhall be
agreed on at a Council, confifting of the
general Officers, with two Commiffion Of-

ficers and two Soldiers to be chosen for each
Regiment, they will not disband or di-
vide, nor suffer themselves to be disbanded
or divided.   And this is one result of that
meeting of the godly obedient Army, this
the fruit of the new Model, and of all the
great undertakings of that man of God (as
his Disciples call'd him) Lieutenant General *Cromwel* in their behalf.

99. They likewise frame there another
submissive business, which they call'd an
humble Representation of the dissatisfaction
of the Army, in relation to the late resolution for so sudden disbanding, where they
are more large in their humble cudgeling of
the Parliament, and do it to that purpose,
with a scorn of all that had been offer'd to
their satisfaction, say, The private Soldiers
will not regard what is behind of Pay after
disbanding, implying all must be had, require further security for the Officers Arrears, as Forest Lands, and the revenues
of Cathedrals, quarrel with the ordinances
past for Indemnity, exemption from Pressing, *&c.* expostulate about the Declaration
against their seditious Petition yet standing
in force, demand reparation for questioning
their mutinous Officers, and will have it a-
gainst those Members of the House who had
done but their duty, and discharg'd their
Consciences in that particular, declare
plain-

plainly, That tho all their Grievances were duly confider'd, it were nothing except thofe perfons were cenfur'd, calling them Men of defperate Principles, Incendiaries, that muft not continue to be their Judges, that is, muft not fit in Parliament, and much more of this nature, which in contempt they fend up to the Houfe. Thefe are they that fight for privilege of Parliament, who have made a Covenant with God and Man fo to do, and well they perform it; thofe they miflike muft be thruft out by head and fhoulders, and fuch as remain, if they be not obedient to them, fhall be ferv'd with the fame fauce: And this is to make a free Parliament. Was there ever a more perfidious breach of Duty, did Rebellion it felf ever outdo it, can any Man think? Yet let us go a little further with them, and we fhall fee greater abominations than thefe.

100. All this while they feem'd to defire only things concerning themfelves, tho very unfittingly and wickedly, both for matter and manner; yet not to meddle with any thing elfe concerning fettling the bufinefs of the Kingdom, which in many Meffages and Declarations they ftill protefted againft, faying (as Sir *Thomas Fairfax* wrote up from *Cambridg*) That whatever was fuggefted or fufpected, they would leave all fuch matters to the wifdom of the

Par-

Parliament. But now *Tempora mutantur,* they have power in their hands, and the Kingdom shall feel it; the Parliament shall not only give them what they will have, but do what they will have done, or smart for it. They make the world believe they will set the King on his Throne and in his Rights, the People in their Liberties, the Parliament in its Duty, and a Golden Age is like to follow.

101. To this end they march up in a hostile way towards *London,* bring his Majesty along with them from *Royston.* Sir *Thomas Fairfax, Cromwel, Ireton,* and the rest of the Officers, write a Letter to the Lord Mayor, Aldermen, and Common Council, telling them, That the sum of what they have desir'd of the Parliament, is a satisfaction to their demands as Soldiers, a reparation upon those that have improv'd advantages (as they falsely say) by false suggestions and misrepresentations to the destruction of the Army, and endeavour'd to engage the Kingdom in a new War. That the things they insist upon as English Men, are a settlement of the Peace of the Kingdom, and of the Liberties of the Subject, which they say they have as much right to demand as their Money, or other common Interest of Soldiers, and that the honest People of *England* are full of the sense of Ruin and Misery,

fery, fhould they disband before. That for the obtaining of thefe things, they are drawing near the City, and declare, That if the City appear not againft them, nor provoke them, they will give no offence; but if they do, they call God to witnefs they are free, and have wafh'd off the Ruin which will befal it : that they will lofe all rather than not be righted of the Men they aim at, therefore defire, that like fellow Subjects and Brethren, the Citizens would follicite the Parliament in their behaf.

102. Here they firft take upon them openly to intermeddle with the bufinefs of the Kingdom, contrary to all the former Declarations and Proteftations ; but their words nor yet their vows were ever any rule to know their meaning by : as *Hammond* told the King concerning *Cromwel,* fo is it with all thofe vifible Saints, have they promis'd, vow'd, fworn never fo much, call'd God and Man to witnefs, if the condition of their Catholick Caufe fo alter, that what they have fo promis'd and fworn be no longer expedient for them, a pretended Enthufiafm, a new Light fhall give a difpenfation, and they will do clean contrary, yet all out of tendernefs of Confcience ; well, they are now in ftrength and power, and will make ufe of it to turn all upfide down.

103. The poor Parliament all this while is sitting upon addle Eggs, take a great deal of pains, like Children, to build Castles of Cards, a puff from their faithful Army blows it all down. It is true, that at first, upon return of their Commissioners, who were sent down to disband, and had brought them an account of the scorn put upon them, how instead of the Regiments coming to the Rendevous appointed, a Command from Sir *Thomas Fairfax* fetch'd them clear another away ; how the train of Artillery was seiz'd upon at *Oxford*, the Money which should have disbanded a Regiment taken away by force, and the Servants whom they had employ'd, beaten and wounded ; this did with good reason startle them ; many of the Members express'd a sharp and severe Sense of it ; the House was taking vigorous and honourable Resolutions, tho oppos'd with might and main by all the Independent Party, who prevail'd but little, being now a known engag'd Faction, till Serjeant Major General *Skippon* stood up, a Presbyterian, one who had seem'd to dislike those factious ways before his last going down to the Army, who was nominated Commander in chief for the Irish Expedition, had receiv'd a gift of a thousand Pounds by way of encouragement to go, but now was willing enough to stay at home with
it;

it; he, forfooth, in a grave way, with a doleful Countenance, and lamentable Voice, makes a long Speech to exhort to moderation, and to bear with the Infirmities of a zealous confcientious Army which had done fo much good Service. Therefore it was his opinion we fhould humble our felves before God, appoint a day of Fafting, and do thofe things which the Army defir'd, give them their full Pay, alter the Ordinance according as they propos'd, and he was perfwaded in his Confcience they would then be fatiffy'd; however they were not to be provok'd, for they were a form'd Body which would be upon us before we were aware. This knockt us on the head, efpecially his laft Argument, a demonftration τȣ οτι; fo it is, they are ftrong, they will fall upon you; timorous Men, as he knew many of thofe were he had to deal with, could make no reply to it.

104. But had he done his duty, given warning of thofe preparations and intentions fooner, when he was below with the Army fo long, and could not choofe but difcern it, the Houfe would not have been fo furpris'd, would have provided againft it in time, but now fear took away the ufe of reafon. They look'd upon the Army as even at their doors, *Hannibal ad portas,* and all of them Children of *Anak,* armed Giants not to be refifted,

105. Whereas in truth there was no such cause of fear. As they in the Army had more Cause carrying about them so much guilt, as I am confident they had as great a share of apprehension. But they presum'd upon their Agents among us, they knew we had them with us both in Parliament and City who would betray us, possess'd with the like evil Spirit as *Ahab*'s Prophets were ; we should prevail, otherwise we were not in so despicable a condition. The Parliament had not yet utterly lost their reputation, the Image of Authority was not wholly defaced in them, they had a stock intire and untoucht of 200000 *l.* provided for disbanding the Army, and service of *Ireland*, multitude of Officers and gallant Soldiers about the Town, who had always fought gallantly, and obey'd readily, had little reason to be in love with the Army which had unhors'd them, so it is likely would have engag'd chearfully and done good service. The City was high in the opinion of the People for courage and resolution, firmness to the Parliament, zeal in the Cause, hatred of Independency, dislike of the Army, and a Purse to make all good, give Sinews and Strength to that side with which they should close, and had particularly presented many Petitions to the House for those very things which they were doing, and the Army only came to undo ;

do ; which were in order to a Peace, restoring the King, settling the Government both
in Church and State, and giving ease and
quietness to the Kingdom, so as they were
in truth already engag'd with us, and waited but a Summons to declare themselves,
when by this unfortunate Man's interposi-
tion at that time (to whom chiefly and to
his Chaplain *Marshal*, we must attribute
all the Evil that has since befallen King and
Kingdom) all was dasht ; instead of a gene-
rous resistance to the insolencies of perfidious
Servants, vindicating the honour of the
Parliament, discharging the trust that lay
upon them to preserve a poor People from
being ruin'd and inslav'd to a rebellious Army, they deliver up themselves and Kingdom to the will of their Enemies, prosti-
tute all to the Lust of heady and violent Men,
suffer Mr. *Cromwel* to saddle, ride, switch,
and spur them at his pleasure.

106. For we instantly fell as low as dirt,
vote the common Soldier his full Pay, the
Officers a Month more (that is in all three
Months) upon disbanding or engaging for
Ireland, take all our Ordinances in pieces,
change and alter them according to their
minds, and (which is worst of all) expunge
our Declaration against that mutinous Petition, cry *Peccavimus* to save a whipping,
but all would not do.

107. In ſo much that when our Commiſſioners were ſent down to the Army at
Triplo Heath, to give an account of our du-
tiful complyance, they would not vouchſafe
to hear them, but when they offer'd to read
the Votes, cry out, Juſtice, Juſtice, a Note
that *Cromwel* and *Ireton* had taught them to
ſing, being done by their directions, as ſome
of their own Diſciples falling out with
them, have ſince diſcover'd; which was by
Mr. *Scawen*, who was one of thoſe were
ſent, reported back to the Houſe, in ſuch a
gaſtly fearful manner (only to terrifie us
and make us more ſupple) he ſaying, the
Army was ſo ſtrong, ſo unanimous, ſo reſolv'd, as the poor Presbyterians hearts fell
an Inch lower, and the Independents made
themſelves merry with it. Then forſooth
the Houſes muſt ſend down Members to a-
bide with the Army as with a Power independent, or a third Eſtate, improve all advantages a ndopportunities, to give good im-
preſſions of the actions and intentions of the
poor Parliament, and, like *Benhadad*'s Servants, catch at any thing of comfort which
might fall; theſe were Sir *Henry Vane* the
younger, Serjeant Major General *Skippon*,
Mr. *Scawen*, and Mr. *Povey*.

108. In the mean time the Army is
marching, draws nearer and nearer to the
City, where, as well as in the Parliament, Men
were

were between hopes and fears; looking upon
what was done sufficient to appeafe them,
what then offer'd, what they always intended
for doing right to the Army; and in truth
to all perfons, they could not but hope as well.
But feeing the poftures and proceedings of the
other fide, there was more caufe of fear, till at
laft that Letter came to the City of which I
fpoke before, which fatisfy'd our doubtings;
and when the Citizens who were fent from
the Common Council brought it to the Parliament, the horror and indignation of fuch
an Impiety, fo great a Prefumption, fo ma-
nifeft a Rebellion, awaken'd us to fee our
danger, and mafter'd thofe fears which had
been given us to awe us from refiftance, fo
as both Houfes and City refolv'd to put
themfelves in a pofture of defence, appointed a Committee of Lords and Commons to
go into the City, call the Committee of the
Militia of *London* to them, and jointly and
feverally do what was neceffary for our common fafety.

109. The Committee went and did their
parts, but they found *Joab*'s hand every
where; the Army had fo plaid *Abfalom*, pretending an intention to fettle Peace immediately, correct the exorbitances with which
the people had been opprefs'd and abus'd,
reftore the King, with fuch other plaufible
things; and their Agents had fo induftri-
oufly

oufly improv'd their Interefts, fome falfe
Brothers in the City, as Alderman *Foulks*,
and Alderman *Gibbs*, fo cunningly wrought
upon mens Minds, fometimes upon their
Fears, fetting out the ftrength and power of
the Army, which threaten'd nothing but
ruin ; fometimes upon their hopes and defires of Peace, gilding over their proceedings, as all done in order to it ; fometimes
upon the diflike of the prefent condition,
affuring them all Taxes and Payments would
by this means be taken off; fometimes upon
their credulity, making them believe, that
thofe Perfons whom the Army had in their
eyes to remove, were not fo well affected to
the publick, but had particular Ends and
Defigns of their own, to arm Reformadoes,
and fet up the power of another Sword to
rule and govern by, fo to continue the
Miferies and Burdens of the People: by
which Falfhoods and Juglings, thofe two
chiefly, like *Jannes* and *Jambres*, had generally bewitcht the City, and lull'd it into a
fecurity, withftanding thofe who had no o-
ther thought than to deliver their Brethren
and themfelves from that fubjection and vaf-
falage to which they were then defign'd,
and are fince brought. As the Citizens refolv'd not to ftir, but look'd on to fee what
this Army would do; fome few did appear, rather to make objection and hinder
the

the bufinefs than help it; and tho many
good orders were made for putting the City
into a pofture to defend it felf, none were
obey'd : fo on all hands the poor Parliament,
and Kingdom, and City it felf were betray'd,
and left to the mercy of the Army, whofe
mercy we fhall foon fee was Cruelty it
felf, Injuftice, Oppreffion, Violence, and
Rebellion in the higheft degree.

110. They now thunder upon us with
Remonftrances, Declarations, Letters, and
Meffages every day, commanding one day
one thing, next day another, making us
vote and unvote, do and undo ; and when
they had made us do fome ugly thing, jeer
us, and fay, our doing juftifies their defiring it, as they ferv'd us concerning all we
had granted for Pay, expunging our Declaration, paffing the Ordinances for Indemnity againft Preffing, and the like.
They tell us in their Reprefentation of the
14*th* of *June*, That our refuming the confideration of thefe things, as to their further
fatisfaction, dos much juftifie their defires
and proceedings fo far ; and therefore they
then proceed further, and fay, They defire
full and equal fatisfaction, not only for themfelves, but for all the Soldiery throughout the
Kingdom, who have concurr'd or will con-
cur with them ; fo ingage all againft the
Parliament, and contract fuch a debt as
                                                      hath

has broken the back of the Commonwealth,
and now say they are not a mercenary Army to serve the arbitrary power of the
State, but that they took up Arms in Judgment and Conscience (notwithstanding
they have receiv'd more Pay than all the
Armies in the Kingdom, and yet liv'd
most of Spoil and free Quarter) therefore
they are resolv'd to assert and vindicate the
power and rights of the Kingdom, and say,
That what they do is short of the proceedings of other Nations, to things of a higher
nature than as yet they had pretended to, in-
stancing in the *Netherlands* and *Scotland*. For
the present they require, that the Houses be
purg'd, those who have appear'd against them
not to be theirs and the Kingdom's Judges, whose names they say they will speedily give in ; they tell the Parliament what
kind of Men they will have preferr'd to
power and trust in the Commonwealth;
then (which was a Crime some six
weeks before, to move in Parliament and
in a Parliamentary way, so as that sagacious
Gentleman Mr *Gurden*, stood up in a rage,
and said it smelt of *Oxford*, and it was much
decryed by all the Crew, but is now of publick merit, and very pious, coming from
their Masters the Army) they will have a
determinate period of time set to this Parliament, some provision to be made for the
con-

continuance of future Parliaments. And when
his Majefty fhall have given his Concurrence to thefe and all other things that fhall
be propos'd for the liberties of the People, the
Militia, and peace of the Kingdom, then
his Rights and of his Pofterity to be confider'd. They will have the Rights of the
People clear'd for freedom of Petitioning,
and fuch as are imprifon'd for pretended
Mifdemeanours to be fpeedily try'd, and
have reparations if they have fuffer'd wrong-
fully; the power given to Committees, and
deputy Lieutenants to be taken into confideration. The Kingdom to be publickly fatisfy'd in point of Accounts, and after publick Juftice done upon fome of the excepted
Perfons, that there be an Act of Oblivion.
Then they conclude that thefe things done,
tho there be many other particulars, yet
(which certainly was merely out of their
great goodnefs and grace, like that of the
modeft Spaniard with his *no quiero mas*) they
will ask no more, but leave the reft to the
wifdom and juftice of the Parliament; and
this they fay they find to be the concurrent
fenfe of the People, by their Petitions prefented to the General, wherein (as in all
the reft) they play the arrant Impoftors and
Mountebanks, being as impudent, falfe,
cunning, bloody, proud, and ambitious as
the Devil himfelf, their grand Mafter.

I They

They will have us believe the Senfe of the People joyn'd with them, and that they petition'd for thefe things; when their own fellow Witches have fince difcover'd how *Cromwel* himfelf drew thofe Petitions, fent them about into the Countries, had his Agents to promote them with mellifluous enamouring promifes (as the expreffion is) fo got fome Independents to fubfcribe them, and perhaps fome few more that they had cozen'd; which ſerv'd the turn, and made their wife General engage himfelf with them, faying, That what he wanted in expreffion of his devotion to their Service, fhould be fupply'd in action, as Mr. *John Lawmind* informs in his *Putney* Projects.

111. The Parliament is now brought to a fine pafs, made a notable free Parliament, but we muft believe it to be fo, becaufe *Cromwel's* Army fays it, and fpeed as well as our firft Parents believing the Serpent, that told them eating the Apple would make them as Gods, wife, and happy. The Army on the other fide triumphs, drives on like *Jehu,* bears down all before it, carries about the King as a Prifoner to fhew him, and make that ufe of him, which the *Philiſtines* would have done with the Ark, prevail againft all oppofition; and truly that and their power together did make them prevail.

112. Their next work charging eleven Perfons, Members of the Houfe of Commons, particularly by name, but with general things ; for particulars they were not provided with, as their friend *John Lawmind* fays, who ufes thefe words, the particular matter of their Charge was to feek after they had in general charg'd them : And another of their Difciples, *Sirrah Nico*, fays, That *Cromwel* confefs'd at *Colebrook*, he had nothing againft Sir *John Maynard*, yet he muft be put in amongft the reft, only becaufe he was a bufie Man againft him and his faction ; fo you fee thefe Thieves falling out fome truth comes to light.

113. With this general Charge there comes another Paper from his Excellency and the Army under his Command, requiring the Members impeach'd may be forthwith fufpended fitting in the Houfe, and a months Pay to be immediately fent down to the Army for a prefent fupply ; and of thefe things to know the refolution by the next Thurfday at the furtheft, which was within two days. They require further, That the Officers who had deferted the Army (as they call'd it, but in truth who had left them for their Rebellion, and engag'd for *Ireland*) fhould have no more of their Arrears paid them till the Army was firft fatisfy'd : And to be fure the Parlia-

ment·

ment fhould have none to defend them,
They command them to raife no new Forces within the Kingdom, nor invite, nor admit any from other parts ; the reafon, or at
leaft the colour for this was, becaufe the
Committee of Safety, at fuch a time as in
obedience to the Order of Parliament they
had endeavour'd to have put the City in a
condition to defend the Parliament and it
felf, had confider'd of raifing fome Force,
but never any thing was put in execution,
nor one Man lifted : And tho the Parliament and City did affure them there was no
proceeding in it, which they might then very likely believe, and in good manners have
acquiefc'd, yet fuch was either their fear,
by reafon of guilt, or their fcorn of the Parliament, and petulancy to fhew how they
flighted what they faid or declar'd, as they
would not believe them, but threap them
down that there was lifting ftill, and quarrel
with them about it, to fuch a height were
they then grown, and others to that tame-
nefs.

114. This pafs'd about the 15th of *June.*
The Houfe took thefe things into confideration, obey'd in all but that concerning the
Members ; wherein they came to a refolution, That upon fuch a general Charge they
could not in Juftice proceed againft them,
nor fufpend them, therefore defire to know
what

what they could charge them with in pa-ticular. They further confider'd how un-handfome it was, the King fhould be fo hurry'd up and down with the Army, and that if he were at fome of his own Houfes near *London*, application might be made to him jointly by them and the Scotifh Com-miffioners, in order to Peace ; whereupon, tho it was mightily oppos'd by the Indepen-dent Party, yet they voted his Majefty fhould be defir'd to come to his Mannor Houfe at *Richmond*.

115. Here the Scholars had broken out a little into rebellion againft their School-mafters the Army, and foon they were lafh'd for it. For on the 23*d* of *June* comes a ratling Leffon, a Remonftrance from his Ex-cellency, full of fharp and fcoffing Expreffi-ons, and ends with a lufty Menace, tells them, *The voting of the King to Richmond* is but in purfuance of the former defign upon him at *Holmby*, and to put his Majefty with-in the reach of thofe Men, who had already lifted confiderable numbers of Horfe and Foot about *London* ; therefore wifhes them, as they tender the welfare of the Kingdom, and the avoiding of jealoufies and other in-conveniencies in the Army, to refume again the confideration of that bufinefs, and not propofe any place for him nearer *London* than they would have the head Quarters of

the

the Army : then to ingratiate themselves with the King and his Party, and make him willing to ftay with them (till their defign was ripe to difpofe of him otherwife, as it was afterwards) they take notice of fome fcandalous information, by the procurement forfooth of eleven Members and others of their Party, as if his Majefty were kept a Prifoner among them, which they fay is moft falfe and contrary to their Principles (as has appear'd fince by what Sir *Thomas Fairfax* commanded to be done to the King in the Ifle of *Wight*, upon his Majefty's anfwer to the four Bills, without order of Parliament, like a great Prince, *Ex mero motu & certa fcientia*, tho it was afterwards approv'd of and juftify'd *Ex parte poft*) but as yet they are harmlefs Saints and good Subjects, all for the King. Therefore they take occafion to declare there, That they defire a juft freedom for his Majefty and thofe of his Party, and profefs they do not fee how there can be a firm Peace, without a due confideration of and provifion for the Rights of himfelf, his Royal Family and late Partakers. O ye Hypocrites, then with Honey for him in their Mouths, and War in their Hearts !

116. For the expunging of the Declaration, they fay, they acknowledg the Juftice of the Houfe in it, but fhould rather have
been

been satisfy'd with the Parliaments declaring how and by whom they had been misinform'd and surpriz'd, and that it is an apparent dishonour to them to pass such a Declaration, and soon after without alteration in the pretended ground and cause of it (for shame of the world) to expunge it : I confess they say true in this, but the old Proverb is, true Jests are bitter Jests.

117. Then for the Members, they insist to have them forthwith suspended upon the general Charge, saying, they would willingly proceed to particulars, if they might be encourag'd by the Justice of the House for suspending them for what it self knows, as having been done there, which they say they cannot prove without breaking the privileges of Parliament : Therefore they advise a necessary expedient for prevention of the like for the future, That in the House of Commons dissenting Members may enter their Dissent, as they do in the House of Peers, with a Protestation, and say, They offer these things from their good wishes to the privileges of Parliament, to render them more lasting by being more innocent.

118. Was ever Parliament so abus'd ? First, they must, because the Army will have it so, give a Judgment upon persons before they know any fault by them, only to encougrage their accusers to tell the fault,

for which that Judgment is already given ;
firſt puniſh, then enquire ; *Hallifax* Law,
and Army Juſtice. And this no leſs than of
ſuſpenſion, where not only the Parties themſelves have a mark of ignominy put upon'em,
are diſpoſſeſt of the execution of that Truſt
which their Country has repoſed in them,
but the places they ſerve for, Towns and
Counties are puniſh'd, depriv'd of their
Repreſentatives in Parliament, and conſe-
quently of their ſuffrages there which they
give by them. Then what muſt this be for ?
even for what was done and ſaid in the
Houſe (for ſo it is laid) contrary to all proceedings and privileges of Parliament,
which will have no man queſtion'd for
that afterwards ; upon this ground, That if
he had done amiſs, the Houſe would at that
time have checkt it ; and they not finding
fault then, for any other to do it, muſt needs
reflect upon their Wiſdom and Integrity, as
if they approv'd of what was ill, or could
not diſcern it. And laſtly, for my young
Maſters to jeer them with their good wiſhes to have their privileges leſs nocent, and
then dare to propound ſo great an alteration
in the very fundamental conſtitution of the
Houſe of Commons, where the minor part
is involv'd in the major, and both make but
one intire Agent in all they do, where
there is no particularizing of perſons, not any
one

one Member to be fo much as nam'd, where all is acted as by one Man, that which muſt bind the whole Kingdom to be eſtabliſh'd by the united conſent of it, there to make ſuch a rent and diviſion as to introduce diſſenting Proteſtations, only to foment Faction and Parties, and by troubling the Fountain, to corrupt all the Streams, is the moſt tranſcending preſumption that ever was heard of.

119. But that which in my opinion carry'd moſt of injuſtice in it ſelf, and diſhonour to the Parliament, was the requiring them to diſcharge and diſperſe thoſe, who upon their orders of invitation and encouragement to engage for *Ireland*, had left the Army, quitted the advantages they might have had in joining in that Rebellion, and wholly caſt themſelves upon the Parliament, as Sir *Robert Pye*'s Men, Colonel *Graves*'s, Colonel *Butlers*, Captain *Farmers*, Lieutenant Colonel *Jackſons*, the Captain, and many of the Soldiers of the Life-Guard, and others quarter'd in *Kent* and *Surry*, the greater part of the two Regiments under Colonel *Herbert* and Colonel *Kempſon*, quarter'd about *Worceſter* and *Eveſham*; theſe honeſt, gallant, faithful, ſtout Men, both Officers and Soldiers, for their obedience to the Parliament, zeal to *Ireland*, muſt be abus'd and ruin'd, the Parliament it ſelf made to eat

its

its own words, break its faith, deceive them who trusted it, deliver them up, make them Anathema's: for what? because the Army says they are Deserters, and raisers of a new War, but in truth, for complying with their Commands, refusing to join in a Rebellion against them, being willing to adventure their lives against the Rebels of *Ireland*.

120. Never was such a violence and scorn put upon a single person, or any society of Men, much less a Parliament, to make it act its own shame and confusion, except by that *Italian*, who to be reveng'd on his Enemy, got him at advantage, bad him deny Jesus Christ, and acknowledg him his Saviour, or he should die presently, which the wretch doing to save his life, he then stabs him to the heart, and says, Go thy ways, I am now reveng'd upon Body and Soul. So the Army threaten'd the Parliament, if all these things foremention'd were not done (and likewise the poor Reformadoes put out of the City, who had offer'd themselves, and were ready to run all dangers for theirs and the City's preservation) and done by the next Thursday night, that then they should be forc'd to take such a course extra-ordinary, as God should enable them and direct them to.

121. And when the Parliament had done it (as they did all but suspending their
Mem-

Members) had retracted that Vote concerning the King's coming to *Richmond* (which the Lords did first at Mr. *Marshal's* earnest sollicitation, as I have heard, who at that time could not have prevail'd so with the House of Commons) prostituting their Honours, renouncing whatever would be of strength and safety to them, casting themselves down naked, helpless and hopeless, at the proud feet of their domineering Masters, it is all to no purpose, it dos but encourage those merciless Men to trample the more upon them, like the Task-masters of *Egypt*, double the tale of their Bricks.

122. For this was a resolution taken, nothing should satisfie, nay not be accepted with a good look, a smile, whilst the eleven Members sat in the House; while *Mordecai* stood in the Gate and bowed not, proud *Haman* cannot be pleas'd, therefore he must die: The eleven Members must out. The House of Commons will not do it, Mr. *Joyce* and his Agitators shall. For this Sir *Thomas Fairfax* takes up his Quarter at *Uxbridg*, some of his Forces advance within three or four Miles of *Westminster*, he sends his Warrants for Provisions into the very Suburbs, a Party of Horse is commanded to be ready at a Rendevouze, to march up to the Parliament, then here is the Case of the eleven Members ; stay, a violence shall be offer'd

up-

upon the Houfe, the Members pull'd out by the Ears, and then *Actum eft de Parliamento,* I may fay *de Parliamentis,* farewel this and all Parliaments.

123. Thofe Gentlemen therefore think it beft, rather than a breach fhould be made upon their occafion, that through their fides the Parliament fhould be ftuck to the very heart, and die for ever, to make it their own act of forbearing the Houfe. And therefore they told the Houfe, they faw they were in that condition they could neither protect them nor themfelves ; that if they would not do as *Achifh* did to *David,* who bid him be gone becaufe the Princes of the Philiftins lov'd him not, yet that they would at their humble fuit and defire be pleas'd to give them leave to withdraw, and to fuch as defir'd it, Paffes to go beyond Sea, which at laft they did agree to, tho truly I muft fay, unwillingly ; but which all faid, they look'd upon it as a good Service done to the Houfe for preventing greater inconveniences.

124. Upon this they forbore, and ftaid, I think, a week or better, expecting if the Army would fend in a particular Charge a-gainft all or any of them ; which not doing, but inftead of that writing up a Letter to commend their Modefty, they then petition'd the Houfe, that they would fend to the

theArmy to know what particulars they laid
to their charge, and prefix them some convenient time to do it in : Which the House did,
giving them about a week.   And one would
have thought a short day might have serv'd.
That accusing Members in such a manner,
with such a noise, as if they had been so criminous, that as Mr. Sollicitor said by his
Beasts of prey, which were not to have Law
given them, but be knockt in the head, so
they were not worthy of Justice, nor of
privilege of Parliament, nor of common hu-
manity, much less to be us'd with some respect, like Gentlemen who had so long, and
some of them serv'd their Country so often
in Parliament, and more faithfully than e-
ver any of the Army party did, or will do
there or any where else. But all Bonds of duty and civil society must be broken through
to come at their destruction ; they must
needs have known some notorious things by
them which might readily be produc'd.
But it seems they were not so provided, the
particular matter of their Charge was yet
to seek (as their fellow Mr. *John Lawmind*
says) they were then hunting out for Articles, sending about for Witnesses to testifie
any thing, promise, bribe, threaten; but
all would not do: several persons came to
me, informing how they had been follicited
to inform against me ; one *Lewis* told me
they

they had been tampering with him ; one
Westcomb acquainted me how one *Pain* had
been sent for by *Rushworth* his Excellency's
excellent Secretary, to the same purpose,
who lodg'd him in his Chamber, gave him
an Angel the first time ; that he went the second time, and this *Westcomb* with him,
and then had a Horse given him worth ten
Pounds, and the promise of some Place in
the Army, for which it is presum'd he did
some acceptable Service. It seems these
Saints were put hard to it ; well, the first
day pass'd and no Charge came in, they desir'd longer time, and promis'd it should be
ready by such a day, and I think the day after it did come : And if I be not very par-
tial to my self, as in this I believe I am not,
after all this travelling of the Mountains,
out comes *ridiculus Mus.*

125. I will not repeat all the particulars
here, they are in print and our answer
to them, which I hope satisfies all Men ;
besides another answer we put into the
House, more upon the formality of a legal
Plea, which it seems satisfy'd them, for
they never proceeded further, nor did the
Army prosecute, but the House order'd the
Speaker to give us Passes according to our de-
sires.

126. I will but make this observation upon some of them, That they and their Party

ty acted thofe very things which they laid to our charge; and what was falfe as to us, was really true in them.

127. One thing was holding a Correfpondency with the King and his Party, which of all Men they ought not to have objected, doing what they did even at that very time; for fuppofe it never fo great a Crime, it ill becomes the Devil to find fault with the Collier for being black: they treat with his Majefty, have fome of his Servants prefent at their Councils of War to debate and prepare things, frame propofals for fettling the whole bufinefs of the Kingdom; and if their own Writers, Prophets of their own, tell true, capitulate for Honours and Preferments, *Cromwel* to have a blew Ribbon, be an Earl, his Son to be of the Bed-Chamber to the Prince, *Ireton* fome great Officer in *Ireland.* Now admit all true they faid of us, was it to be compar'd to this? is it not a *Decimo fexto* to their Folio, a Mole-hill to their Mountain? And I defire it may be taken notice of, that in all the Charge there is not a word of the Plot to fetch the King from *Holmby*, bring him to *London*, or put him at the head of the Army, which they made the groundwork of all their Villanies, pretending fome of us (in truth underhand, and in their Pamphlets naming me) to have had fuch an intention; and

and that what they did was by way of prevention. Is it likely this would have been o-
mitted if there had been the least colour of
truth for it ? but Truth was what they ever
least look'd after in all their Speeches and
Actions, caring only to serve a turn, gain an
advantage by cozening the world, and then
cast about how to make it good by power,
or amuse Men with some new Cheat, that
the last might be forgotten.

128. They accuse us of infringing, and
endeavouring to overthrow the Liberties and
Rights of the Subject in arbitrary and op-
pressive ways, and by indirect and corrupt
practices to delay and obstruct Justice.
These are the words in their general Charge.
Now I appeal to all Men, and even to their
own Consciences, who say this, whether of
the two, they or their Party, or we in the
House of Commons , upon all occasions,
were for violence, oppression, and ruin, to
destroy all that came before them, sequester
Estates, impose great Fines, imprison, starve,
sometimes take away life, make Men offenders for a word, make all advantages, wrest
and strain up to the height of all their penal
Ordinances ; and who they were that had
the hand in making all those penal Ordinances, so severe for Sequestrations, so high for
Compositions, so insnaring and bloody for
making new Treasons, and little things to
be

be capital Crimes; that no Man almoft was fafe, free from queftion, and few or none queftion'd but fure to be deftroy'd. How many Minifters were pull'd out of their Livings for very fmall faults? how many Perfons made Delinquents, their Eftates torn in pieces, themfelves, their Wives and Children turn'd to beggery, and ready to ftarve for no great offences, at leaft that for which they did not deferve fo fevere a punifhment? What Committees were fet up? That of Haberdafhers Hall, to pill and poll Men, put them to an Oath as ill as that *ex officio* to make them difcover their Eftates, and expofe themfelves to their mercilefs carving out a fifth and twentieth part, which was the undoing of many, even fetching in fome of the Members of the Houfe to whom they had a difpleafure, and generally all Men who had crofsd or oppos'd them in any thing: that of Goldfmiths Hall, to impofe Fines to the ruin of many of the beft Families of *England*: that of Sequeftrations, where the very intention of the Houfes was perverted, that Committee being firft propos'd and made only for great and notorious Offenders, but afterwards came to be worfe than any Spanifh Inquifition, few efcaping that were ever queftion'd; I dare fay Serjeant *Wild* the Chairman, and Mr. *Nicklis* the Lawyer, and fome few more Bloodhounds, who always

at-

attended there, never gave their Votes for
the freeing of scarce any one person; and then
the delay there is worse than the condemna-
tion, making suitors wait one, two years,
and commonly be sequester'd at last. The
Committee of Examinations where Mr.
Miles Corbet kept his Justice Seat, which
was worth something to his Clerk, if not to
him, what a continual Horse Fair it was?
even like Dooms-day it self, to judg persons of all sorts and sexes.

129. Did not that Faction put on all
these things? did not we still oppose, hinder
it all we could? how earnestly and how often have we mov'd the putting down those
Committees? that of Sequestration, that of
Haberdashers Hall. Those in the Counties
sometimes got orders of the House for that
purpose, brought in Ordinances, and still
by some art or other of theirs put by when it
was thought in a manner settled, so as the Government might have return'd to Sheriffs,
Justices of Peace, Grand Juries, and other
Ministers of Justice in that subordination
which the Law had establish'd. Was any
preserv'd and deliver'd out of his trouble,
that we or some of us had not a hand in it?
Were we not call'd the moderate Party?
branded with that Title (for they held it a
crime) were we not said to favour Malignants? when in truth we had respect to the
Par-

Parliament, that it fhould not be made the Inftrument of thofe mens Lufts, and contract that Odium which only could ruin it, and upon which this very Party, being themfelves the caufe of it, took the advantage to mafter and fubdue it, they in the beginning of their Rebellion exclaiming againft the Parliament for thofe things, and therewith poffeffing the Country, which themfelves and their Faction made it do: Who but they drew all bufinefs into the Parliament, efpecially when themfelves or their Friends were any thing concern'd? And had they not an Art of delaying men, and making them attend when they could not mifchiefthem by difpatching the bufinefs? were any more violent in an arbitrary way of proceeding than they? nay, were any fo but they? could a Mayor, or Officer, or a Burgefs for Parliament be chofen almoft in any Town of *England*, but with their leaves and according to their likings? And on the other fide, did not we prefs to have all things left to the Law of the land, and to the antient and ordinary courfe? yet they accufe us to be the troublers of *Ifrael*, and themfelves would be thought to be the reftorers, juft as the Wolf in the Fable charg'd the Lamb with troubling the Waters.

130, They charge us befide with having a great power upon the Treafure of the

King

Kingdom, difpofing of the publick Monies, inriching our felves, and fay in many of their Declarations, that we would embroil the Land in a new War, that we might not be called to an account for them. O the impudence! They know that themfelves only and their Creatures had power over the Monies, and medled in Money matters, well licking their Fingers; for they know they fhar'd and divided amongft themfelves all the Fat of the Land, the Treafure, the Offices, the King's Revenue, the Revenue of the Church, the Eftates of fo great a part of the Nobility and Gentry, whom they had made Delinquents, and we, not one of us had any thing to do in all this; Mr. Recorder I think only was of the Committee of the King's Revenue, but very feldom came thither. And did not they make ufe of the price in their hands? And did they not like charitable perfons begin at home, give Gifts and Offices to all their own Party, to fome upon mere Grace, as the thoufands to Mr. *Blaxton*, a thoufand Pound to Mr. *Pury* (befides a good Office) as much to Mr. *Hodges* of *Glocefterfhire*, to Alderman *Pennington*, who had conceal'd three thoufand Pounds of Sir *John Pennington*'s which he had in his hands, for which, by their ordinance, he fhould have forfeited the treble, and had he been a friend to the eleven Members
bers

bers should not have been spar'd ; they did not only forgive him that, but gave him that three thousand Pounds, and three thousand Pounds more, which was upon the City's turning him out of their Militia, and presently made him be put in again. The Speaker had Money given him, I know not how much, 6000 *l.* at one time (as I remember) was made Master of the Rolls, Chancellor of the Dutchy, and a good while Keeper ; Mr. Sollicitor was, besides his being Sollicitor, the King's Attorny, and about two years one of the Lord Keepers, got infinitely by the Pardons upon Compositions, which was a device only to fill his Coffers, and had a thousand Pounds given him at the expiration of his Commission for the Great Seal. So had all his fellow Commissioners, Mr. *Brown*, Mr. *Prideaux*, and Serjeant *Wild*, each their thousand Pound besides the profits of the Seal ; Mr. *Prideaux* also made himself Post-master of *England*, being but the Chairman of a Sub-Committee to the Grand-Committee of Grievances, where my Lord of *Warwick* and *Burlamachi* were contesting about the place, which was there represented as a publick Grievance, tho my Lord of *Warwick*'s Grant prov'd not to be so ; but this worthy Gentleman being one of the Committee, and in the Chair, who was to hear both , and report their

K 3 Ca

Cases to the Grand Committee, from whence it was to come to the House, finding it a convenient Employment, worth some 24, or 2500 *l. per Annum*, eas'd them of it, took it himself, and has kept it ever since. Mr. Serjeant *Wild* was trusted with some Money by the Lady *Thornborough*'s Father for the use of his Daughter, and took occasion upon her going to *Oxford*, pretending she had got possession of his Estate, to get a fair Ordinance of both Houses to have that Money given to himself; but sure found some good Law for it, as he did for hanging of Captain *Burley*; and being excellent at it, no question would find Law to hang the eleven Members, were there a whole dozen of them, and me highest for writing this, which he would prove to be a greater Treason than any in the Statute of the 25*th* of *Edward* the 3*d*; and when I come within his power, I will forgive it him, let him hang as many, and get as much of the Commonwealths Money as he can in the mean time. But I will say this for him, the Elders of *Jezreel* that found a Law to put *Naboth* to death, were but fools to him. Then how many of their small Prophets were prefer'd, that Man of Conscience Alderman *Hoil*, that worthy Lawyer Mr. *Nicklis*, Sir *William Allison*, Mr. *Love*, Mr. *Lenthal* the Speaker's Son, these two made six Clerks; Mr.

Mr. *Lisle*, Master of St. *Cross's*, Mr. *Miles Corbet*, Colonel *White*, a Colonel that never was in the Field with his Regiment, Mr. *Allen* the Goldsmith ; all of them, and I know not how many more, in places of great profit, some in the Courts of *Westminster*, others made Treasurers of their Armies, as *Allen* and *White* ; the latter also made Clerk of the Assizes in the Northern Circuit, worth 5 or 600 *l. per Annum. Cromwel* has 2500 *l. per Annum*, Sir *Peter Wentworth* a Gentleman's Estate for half the value, settled likewise by Ordinance, tho the Gentleman (whose delinquency was perhaps aggravated, because he would not sell him that Land which he had long desir'd, like *Naboth*'s Vineyard) offer'd to pay the Money to the State as the Fine for his Composition, which by the rules of their own proceedings could not in Justice have been deny'd him. I remember we put by the Ordinance two or three times, but I hear it is since past, which makes me mention it here.

131. To some for reparation of Losses. So Mr. *Cornelius Holland*, who had some inferiour place in the Prince's Houshold (which certainly he was not born to, the height of his ambition reaching no further in the beginning than to be Sir *Henry Vane*'s Man) was in recompence set over the

King's

King's Children, above my Lady of *Dorset*, and had the managing of their Houshold some three or four years; then they gave him the King's Pastures in *Buckinghamshire* for twenty one years, worth to him *de claro* some 15 or 1600 *l. per Annum.* Sir *William Strickland* for the burning of his House in *Yorkshire*, has a Gentleman's Estate in *Kent* of a good value. Mr. *Henry Herbert* had 3000 *l.* given him out of my Lord of *Worcester*'s Woods, and Sir *John Winter*'s. The Lord *Say*, in lieu of the Mastership of the Wards, which by his power since the beginning of this Parliament he had wrested from the Lord *Cottington*, had 10000 *l.* and for part of the Money (I think 4000 *l.* of it) had *Hanworth* House, with the Lands about it, which was worth, as they say, 14000 *l.* Colonel *Fleetwood* was by way of Sequestration put into the Remembrancers place of the Court of Wards, which his Brother held, and by going to *Oxford* lost it; upon the putting down of the Court he had 3000 *l.* recompense: multitudes there are more of this kind.

132. To some for pretended Arrears; as to Sir *Arthur Haslerig* 7000 *l.* who had earn'd it well at the *Devizes* and *Cherrington.* To the Lord *Fairfax,* Sir *William Constable,* Sir *William Brereton,* great Sums. To Colonel *Thompson* 2000 *l.* for his wooden Leg, which

which nothing but a Cannon could have helpt him to, for he would never come within Musket fhot. To Colonel *Purefoy* and his Son Colonel *Bofwel*, fome 1500 *l.* each; and fo to many more.

133. To fome to buy their Voices, make them Profelytes. To Mr. *Wefton*, Son to the Earl of *Portland*, the reviving an arrear of a Penfion which was his Ladies, and if I be not deceiv'd, had been difcontinu'd for many years : The Debenter, as I remember, was 4000 *l.* To the Lord *Grey* of *Groby* (who had before been zealous for my Lord of *Effex*, as he had good reafon for the refpeĉts he had receiv'd from him) a confiderable Sum, which I well remember not, to be paid him out of fuch difcoveries of Delinquents Eftates as he fhould make ; whereupon he and his Terriers were long attending the Committee of Examinations, in the profecution ftill of fome Game or other, till his Sum was made up. To Mr. *Scawen*, one who formerly had not very well lik'd of their ways, 2000 *l.* How many of the Lords that could not be heard before, nor their Petitions fcarce vouchfafed to be read, when they tackt about and voted with them, were then prefently confider'd, and good proportions allow'd them ; nay, they were fo impudent as fome of them would not ftick to give it for a reafon openly in the Houfe, why

why they would not grant their defires,
that they took notice how they gave their
Votes : Mr. *Gourden* is the Man I have heard
fay fo feveral times ; this was an excellent
way to make a free Parliament, for the Members to be honeft and difcharge their Confciences.

134. Then for Accounts ; I would fain
know what Accounts they have pafs'd : Let
any Man perufe my Lord *Fairfax*'s and Sir
William Conftable's, I hear they are ftrange
ones for the great Sums they have finger'd :
And I am fure the Committee of Accounts
did complain, that their Sub-Committees
were beaten in *Staffordfbire*, where Mr.
Purefoy and Mr. *Bofwel* fhould have acted,
and would not.

135. Upon the whole matter, I would
have our Accufers fay fo much by one of us :
I confefs, I am forry to difcover this of them,
it being much againft my nature, but I am
forc'd to it for my vindication. I may fay
with the Apoftle, They have compell'd me,
and not only fo to recriminate, but even to
glory a little in fome thing. Have any of us
ever refus'd to account, who were liable to
it ? Sir *William Lewis* did account for the
Monys he receiv'd, being Governor of *Portf-
mouth,* fo fairly and fatisfactorily, as that
the Committee of Accounts made a fpecial
report of it to the Houfe, to be (as they
                                                        faid)

ſaid) an Example to others for his care and juſt dealing in managing the States Monies which came to his hands. Major General *Maſſey* I am ſure was ſollicitous to perfect his accounts, which if or no he had done before they drove him away I know not. Sir *William Waller* and Colonel *Long* finiſh'd theirs. Sir *Philip Stapleton* never touch'd but his perſonal Pay, yet did account, and had but forty Shillings a day, being Lieutenant General of the Horſe under my Lord of *Eſſex*, who was Generaliſſimo, when Sir *Arthur Haſlerig* had five Pounds for commanding the Horſe under Sir *William Waller*, a Place inferior to his, and had been at no charge, having liv'd ſtill upon Sir *William Waller*, and gotten well all along the Imployment. Sir *William Waller* had his Arrears after his ſubordinate Officer; Sir *Arthur* had led the way, who broke the Ice for his General and all the reſt. Sir *Philip Stapleton* had alſo his, a very ſmall one for ſo eminent an Officer, in regard his allowance was no greater; it came to about 1700 *l.* having left the benefit of his whole Eſtate during all the Wars, which *Haſlerig* did not, if his Neighbours in *Leiceſterſhire* ſay true, that his Grounds have continu'd full ſtock'd all this while, better than ever they were before, ſo ſafe and well protected (as I have heard) that his Neighbours when there was danger,

would

would fend their Cattel thither; I confefs, I underftand not the myftery.

136. Here is all concerning matters of Accounts and Arrears of the eleven Members, the reft medled not with any of the States Monies, fome of them have refus'd to receive what the Houfe had given them upon much jufter grounds than all the pretences of the others that had fo much. I my felf for my Sufferings after the Parliament 3*d. Car.* which continu'd many years, coft me fome thoufands of Pounds, and prejudic'd me more, had five thoufand Pounds given me by the Houfe for my reparation. I refus'd it, and faid, I would not receive a Penny till the publick debts were paid. Let any of them fay fo much. I defire who ever fhall chance to read this, to pardon me this folly, I do not mean for not taking the Money, but feeming to boaft of it. I muft again repeat the Apoftle's words, I am become a Fool in glorying, but they have compel'd me. It is true, I had paid for a Fine impos'd in the King's Bench, which I laid down in ready Money out of my Purfe, a thoufand Marks: This in the time of thefe troubles, when my whole Eftate was kept from me in the Weft, that for three years or thereabouts I receiv'd thence not one Farthing, was reimburs'd to me.

137. Now I appeal to the world, whether our accufers, or we the poor eleven Members, fo decry'd, fo opprefs'd, were the more guilty, who they were, who had gotten, cozen'd, opprefs'd, were indeed the Traitors. If he did not fay as truly as he did wittily, if they had not had more men than matter againft us, they had been the Traitors themfelves, which many of their own Difciples have upon the matter confefs'd and publifh'd, faying, they were to feek for matter; only we were a Beam in their Eyes: And their great Apoftle *Lilburn* himfelf fays, the great aim was but to pull down thofe who ftood in the way of their preferment.

138. Here is our Crime, I will ask pardon of God for my failings, even in the performance of all thefe duties, where I ferv'd my Country beft, but not of the Parliament from whence I defire no favour. Let them put upon me the fevereft difquifition, either concerning thofe things then charg'd, or the great Treafon fince committed, of endeavouring to defend my felf, the Parliament, the City, from a rebellious, unjuft, oppreffing Army, which againft all Laws of God and Man, came to force us, for which I ftand voted to be impeach'd of Treafon, and am outed the Houfe, of which I fhall treat prefently.

139.

139. But firft I fhall fhew the Steps to it.
The Army now did all, the Parliament was
but a Cypher, only cry'd Amen to what
the Councils of War had determin'd. They
make themfelves an abfolute third Eftate,
have Commiffioners refiding with them
from the Parliament, Agents from his Majefty, and abufe both fufficiently; as folemn-
ly treated with as if no Subjects, but a Body fubordinate to neither, vefted with an
Independent Authority, claiming only from
God and their Sword. The whole bufinefs of
the Kingdom is there now agitated, and the
engagement of the Army is the Standard by
which all propofitions muft be meafur'd. If
any thing be offer'd by the Parliament which
they like not, it is prefently anfwer'd not
to ftand with their folemn Engagement.
Many meetings there were, great confultations and debates upon certain propofals for
fettling of a Peace, and fecuring the Rights
and Liberties of the People.

140. Notwithftanding this, while thefe
things are in agitation, after all their affronting, baffling, forcing the Parliament, marching up againft it and the City, contrary to
their orders, by which they were not to
come nearer than within forty Miles of *London*, they will have them own them for
their Army, undertake to provide for their
maintenance, and immediately fend down

a months Pay, yet will not be subject to them in any thing. All this is done, Mr. *Marshal* the Minister being a principal Instrument for them, who was still going and coming between *Westminster* and the head Quarters, or at the Parliament doors solliciting the Members of both Houses, perswading them by all manner of arguments, sometimes assurances, sometimes terrifyings, to agree to those things which the Army desir'd; and this not in order to the setting up of Presbytery, in which he had formerly been so zealous (for the Presbyters were not then Trump, and he meant to whine therefore to put out them to take in better Cards for his turn) Afterwards they send to repeal the Ordinance for the Militia of *London*, which had been settled upon many and long debates, to stand for one whole year, and renew the former expir'd Ordinance for establishing the old Committee, which was the year before.

141. It is but ask and have, that is presently done; and truly I think it was a design of the Army, merely to provoke the City, engage them to do something, express a dislike perhaps, fly out, and give them an occasion to offer some violence should they persist; or if yield after a little ill favour'dly shewing their teeth, then to put such things upon them, so yoke them,

break

break their ſtrength, trample upon their Liberties and Privileges, as they ſhould not be able afterwards upon any occaſion to raiſe them diſturbance, and make oppoſition to whatever they ſhould ſet on foot, tho never ſo grievous and diſpleaſing to the whole Kingdom; for they thought not themſelves ſecure whilſt the City ſtood unbroken.

142. Their Plot took, the City was very much mov'd at this ſudden Act of the Houſes, in the altering their Militia, without ſo much as giving them notice to hear what they could ſay in a point ſo nearly concerning them.   They look upon it as an Infringement of their Charter (granted and confirm'd to them by ſo many Kings ſucceſſively, by which they were ſtill to have the power of their own Militia) as a ſhaking of the foundation of all their ſecurity for thoſe vaſt ſums of Money they had lent, which depended only upon Ordinances: and the eaſie and ſudden repealing of this, gave them cauſe to fear they might be ſerv'd ſo in the reſt.

143. Whereupon at their Common Council they agreed upon a Petition to the Houſes, informing them of the diſtempers in the City upon the change they had made, and beſeeching them to reeſtabliſh it as it was before; which was preſented by
the

the Sheriffs, fome of the Aldermen, and of the Members of the Common Council in a fair and fubmiffive way. But the Parliament durſt do nothing without the leave of their Maſters, only give them good words, and fo hop'd to ſlide over the buſineſs. Then fome young Men, Apprentices and others, appear'd, preffing hard, who would not be ſatisfy'd till it was done ; which the Houſes ſticking at, the young Men infiſting, drew a great concourſe of people, putting things into fome heat, fo as at laſt they prevail'd, and the Militia was again ſettled according to their deſire : upon which they went away returning to their homes, only fome of the younger and more unruly ſort remain'd, among whom fome idle people (and perhaps not well affeĉted)Soldiers and others, and I have heard fome of the Independents even belonging to the Army, thruſt themſelves, and put the multitude, diſorderly enough before, into great diſtempers, who then would make the Houſes do this and the other thing, vote the King's coming to *London*, the calling in of the eleven Members, and I know not what elſe, would not ſuffer the Parliament Men either of the one Houſe or the other, to ſtir till all was voted and paſs'd which they defir'd, keeping them there till I think nine of the clock at night ;

L   when

when the Common Council hearing of these
disorders, sent down the Sheriffs of *London*
and some of the Aldermen to appease them,
which they did. This was upon Monday
the 26*th* of *July*. The Houses adjourn'd
themselves, the House of Peers to Friday,
the Commons house to the next day. The
City had against the next day, which was
Tuesday, taken order to prevent such further inconveniences by unruly people af-
sembling about *Weſtminſter*, which before
they could not well do, in regard their Militia was unsettled by the alteration that the
new Ordinance upon the Armies command
had made, and I heard sent down a Message
to the House of Commons to assure them of
it; but Mr. Speaker was so hasty to adjourn
till the Friday, perhaps because the rather
he would not receive that Message which
had half spoil'd the Plot, that he would scarce
stay till it was a House; and some of the factious crying to adjourn, he did so, tho many
cry'd out against it, who could not be
heard.

144. By the Friday the two Speakers,
the Earl of *Mancheſter* of the Peers, and Mr.
Lenthal of the Commons, instead of giving
their attendance according to their duty upon the Houses, with eight Lords and fifty
eight

eight Commoners, were run down to the Army, there enter into an engagement, bearing date the 4th of *August*, to live and die with it, upon pretence of a force and violence to the Parliament, but in truth by a Conspiracy with the Army, defign'd and laid principally by Mr. *Saint John* the Sollicitor, as appears by a Letter fent from *Rufbworth*, Sir *Thomas Fairfax*'s Secretary, to the Speaker, with no name in it, but the latter part of it written with his own hand, advifing him not to appear at the Houfe on Friday morning, but to take counfel of Mr. Sollicitor, who would tell him what was fit to be done, affuring him the Army would all lie in the dirt or protect them who were their friends. This, as I remember, was the effect of the Letter, yet remaining in one of the Houfes; which, no doubt, came from Sir *Thomas Fairfax*, and Mr. *Cromwel*, and the reft of thofe Governors undertaking fo for the Army, and fhews who was the man that muft give the Orders, and direct what was to be done by the Houfe, and then may well be fuppos'd to be the Author of all. The ground of this Engagement is made to be a Declaration of the Armies fhewing the reafons of their advance towards *London*, as full of falfhood as it is of malice againft the eleven poor Members, and in truth intended only againſt them, who are by it ſaid to be the cauſe of all that had been done in the City ; that therefore they were reſolv'd to march up to *London*, expecting the well affected people of the City would either put us in ſafe cuſtody, or deliver us up to them, ſtuffing up the whole Declaration with falſhoods and lies, as well in the narrative part as in the comment upon it ; they pretend, That to carry on our former evil deſigns, and preſerve our ſelves from the hand of Juſtice, we had endeavour'd to caſt the Kingdom into a new War, and to that end had procur'd an under hand liſting of Reformadoes, and continu'd a wicked and treaſonable Combination, which we caus'd ſeveral perſons to enter into, That this could not be done in the time of the old Commiſſioners for the Militia, and therefore the new were made, who many of them were very intimate with us, which was a juſt cauſe for the Army to have them chang'd again : That thereupon the tumult was abetted and fomented by us to violate the Parliament, and force it into our hands, which makes them require that we may be in that manner deliver'd up; and declar'd all that was done in the Houſes that day or afterwards, till thoſe fugitive Members ſhould return again, null and void (ſo here the Army

takes

takes upon it to declare what Votes fhall
ftand good, what not ; and this is for the
honour and freedom of the Parliament, that
which thofe worthy Patriots would live and
die upon) And befides, they fay they were
labouring after the fettlement of the Kingdom, and had even brought it to perfewill be,
the particular propofals ready to be fent to
the Parliament for a final conclufion of all
our troubles ; which conclufion of our troubles, in truth, nothing in the fight of Man
could have hinder'd, but this curfed practice
of violence upon the Parliament, which very thing in them was as curfed a High Treafon as could be committed, a mercenary Army rais'd by the Parliament, all of them
from the General (except what he may have
in expectation after his Father's death) to
the meaneft Centinal, not able to make a
thoufand Pounds a year Lands, moft of the
Colonels and Officers mean Tradefmen, Brew-
ers, Taylors, Goldfmiths, Shoemakers, and the
like ; a notable Dunghil, if one would rake
into it, to find out their feveral Pedigrees :
thefe to rebel againft their Mafters, put conditions upon them, upon the King and whole
Kingdom, make their Will a Rule, that all
the Interefts of King, Parliament, and
Kingdom muft be fquared by, which they
are not afham'd to declare here to the world.

145. And this pious Declaration do thefe worthy Lords and Commons receive with much approbation, and with much thankfulnefs to God in the firft place, and next under him to the ever faithful Army; and fo became, like the Profelites which the Scribes and Pharifees made, twofold more the Children of Hell than themfelves, more criminous, and guilty of a greater Treafon, as having broken a higher Truft, being themfelves part of the Parliament which they deferted and betray'd; a wound given in the more noble and vital parts, tearing the Bowels, and piercing to the very Heart. Whereas the Army were but Servants, outward and minifterial parts, fo to be look'd upon, and fo punifh'd; Slaves were crucify'd, but Citizens that betray'd were exterminated, they and their pofterity, and the whole City turn'd into mourning, fenfible of the lofs as the Body when depriv'd of a principal Member.

146. They fhould have remembred, that even at the time of the pretended force which they would have men believe to have driven them away, the Houfe lay under a greater force, and themfelves were greater Slaves to the lufts of the Army which trampled
up-

upon their Necks, made them more contemptible than the smalleft Court of Guard that had but a Corporal to command it, to eat their words, their Declarations, Orders, Ordinances, break their Faith, betray and deſtroy all that ſerv'd them faithfully, give thanks for being cudgel'd and abus'd, pray and pay, and be glad it would be accepted; ſhould not every Member have been ſenſible of ſuch violations and injuries done to the Body? But ſome will ſay it was as theſe Men will have it, who were like the ſinful luſts in the Soul, quiet and well pleas'd, while the ſtrong man the Devil keeps the houſe: So they were ſatisfy'd with all that was done, becauſe it was according to their Minds, conducing to their Ends. If it be ſo, and that they will be Slaves, let them be Slaves ſtill, for they deſerve no better. The Army was the fitteſt place for them, as *Brutus* ſaid of thoſe he took Priſoners at the firſt Battel of *Philippi*, Let them go, ſays he, they are greater Captives in their own Camp under *Ceſar* and *Anthony* than here.

147. They might likewiſe have conſider'd, that the force upon the Parliament from the Army, as it was greater, ſo to have been a more horrid crime, of more dangerous conſequence to the Kingdom, and

L 4   more

more deftructive to the being of Parliaments than that from the Apprentices; which is, in my opinion, very clear. This of the Apprentices being a fudden tumultuary thing of young idle people without defign, and without that obligation; indeed but an effect of the other, both as following their example, and alfo as occafion'd by the juft offence which they had given the City: whereas the Army was a form'd deep laid defign of revenge upon them they call'd their Enemies, of domination over the Parliament and Kingdom, carry'd on both with power and cunning, laying the foundation of a perpetual Tyranny by a company of hir'd Servants, that had receiv'd more wages ten times than their work deferv'd, and now betray'd the truft repofed in them, rifing againft their Mafters, whofe own Swords they turn'd upon their breafts, to force them to do moft difhonourable, unjuft, infamous actions, deliver up themfelves and the Kingdom to their wills. So as take the act of the Apprentices at the worft, it is *ex malis minimum*, and that of thofe fugitive Members at the beft, which is, that they were really under a force, and under a fear, they did *vitare Charibdim incidere in Scyllam*, and leap (as the old Proverb is) out of the Fryingpan into the Fire, wherein they were unfortunate;

*

fortunate; and well would it be for them in the day of their accounts if it were but fortune, but it is too apparent to have been in some of them a propens'd Malice and detestable Combination.

148. As for what they lay to the eleven Members, with all the aggravations in that Declaration, I will not answer it as Mr. *Nathaniel Fines* did Mr. *Walker*'s Charge against him, to say only thou liest, and quote along the Margin, First, Second, Third, and Fourth Lie. But this I will say to disprove it, affirming it upon the word of a Gentleman, and faith of an honest Man (I think I may speak as much for the whole number) I was not in the City all the time those businesses were in agitation, knew nothing of the Petitions nor actings in the Common Council, nothing of the City's engagement, never saw it till two or three days after it was printed, had not the least thought of the Apprentices coming down to *Westminster*, nor notice of it till the very day at eleven of the Clock when they were already there. We had appointed four days before to meet that day at dinner at the Bell in *Kingstreet*, there to even our Reckonings, because we had made a common Purse for Lawyers Fees and other charges,

in

in preparing our anſwer for the Houſe, then to take our leaves one of another, reſolving to go ſeveral ways, ſome beyond Sea, ſome into the Country.   As I was going into my Coach (there was with me Sir *Philip Stapleton*, Sir *William Waller*, Major General *Maſſey*, and Mr. *Long)* one brought us word of the hubbub at the Houſe, whereupon we reſolv'd not to go, and parted companies upon it ; but preſently Sir *William Lewis*'s Footman came to tell us, his Maſter and Mr. *Nichols* were ſtaying for us at the Bell ; upon which Sir *Philip Stapleton*, Sir *William Waller*, and my ſelf (who were yet together) went thither, but hearing more of the diſorder about *Weſtminſter-Hall*, we would not ſtay ſo much as to make an end of our Dinners, but preſently came away. I mention this particular becauſe I know they have made a great matter of that meeting, as if it was to be near hand, to receive information, and ſend inſtructions according to occaſion, when we were as innocent of it as any of thoſe who cry out moſt againſt us ; nay more, if it be true what is ſo confidently reported, as I ſaid before, that there were Independents moſt buſie amongſt that unruly multitude.

149. Here we have ſeen what thoſe worthy

thy Members did at the Army, and upon what ground, and befides what little reafon they had to go away upon the pretended force, which was a fudden thing, then paft, and care taken it fhould be no more, and they lying before under a greater force, which they purpofely now ran again into, to continue it the longer upon themfelves and the Kingdom. Now let us fee what in the mean time was doing at *London*.

150. The Houfes met according to the adjournment upon Friday the 30*th* of *July,* fome fix or fevenfcore in the Houfe of Commons, and as great a number of Lords in their Houfe as of thofe who went to the Army, but all mute, neither having their Speaker, for whom they fent about to feek, waiting till they had certain information how they had difpos'd of themfelves; then they fell into confideration of what was to be done, and that offer'd it felf, which in truth was obvious to every man's reafon, to chufe other Speakers. For the Lords Houfe there could be no queftion, it was every day's practice, their Speaker being but *pro tempore,* and changeable at pleafure; fo they make choice of my Lord *Willoughby* of *Parham.* For the Houfe of Commons, it lay not fo above ground, their Speaker being a

fet-settled Officer, made with great Formalities, and not fo moveable at pleafure; but that he cannot be at all remov'd upon no occafion, not for mifdemeanour (as it is not efteem'd for a Speaker to be honeft, or to be fo powerful by his compliance with the major or the more active part of the Houfe, to be born out in his Knaveries, as fome have the luck of it) or if he defert the Houfe as Mr. *Lenthal* lately did, or be difabled by ficknefs, or any other accident, I think no Man will fay. For then what Act of continuance will be of avail to keep up the Parliament, fince it would depend upon the will of one Man, or the uncertainty of his health, to fruftrate all fuch provifions, and at any time to fet a period to a Parliament?

151. Therefore they proceed to the choice of their Speaker, and pitch upon Mr. *Henry Pelham,* who, according to the cuftom, is prefented at the Lords Houfe Bar, brought in by my Lord of *Pembrook* in his Robes, and there receiv'd.

152. They then go on upon the bufinefs of the Houfe, take into confideration the Letter fpoken of fent by *Rufhworth* to Mr. *Lenthal* the late Speaker, which difcover'd the intention of the Army to march up a-

againſt

gainſt the City ; whereupon they order a Letter to be written to the General, ſigni-fying in what quietneſs they ſat, and that therefore he ſhould not advance his Quarters any nearer.

153. They afterwards order the eleven Members to come and give their attendance, who were preſently ſent for, and ſome o-thers that had been forc'd by the Army to forbear the Houſe.

154. For amongſt other enormous pro-ceedings of the Army, one was, upon pre-tence that ſome ſat there who had born Arms againſt the Parliament, or abetted the other ſide, they make the Houſe enjoin ſome Gentlemen to preſent a ſtate of their Caſe upon certain Votes then paſs'd, which put an incapacity upon ſuch as were com-prehended in them under a heavy penalty if they forbore not the Houſe of themſelves, ſo compelling them either to accuſe them-ſelves againſt all rule of Juſtice, and the ve-ry law of Nature, undergoing the greateſt hazard that could be ; for if they fail'd in a tittle, as very well one might in a thing done three or four years before, or that any Knave would come and ſwear ſomething a-gainſt him, they underwent the penalty,

or

or elfe to deprive themfelves of their rights of fitting in the Houfe, and fo the Town or County which had chofen him lofe the fervice of their Burgefs or Knight; indeed this was a heinous villany, but they are guilty of fo many that one drowns another.

155. They pafs a Vote, that the King may be humbly defir'd to come to his own houfe at *Richmond*, that fo the Houfes of Parliament and Commiffioners of *Scotland* might have accefs to him, to propofe what was neceffary for fettling the Peace of the Kingdom, himfelf be in a place of fafety out of the hands and power of the Army, whofe fair fhews towards him they had caufe to fufpect to be no other than the kiffes of *Judas*, to betray and ruin both him and the Kingdom: and accordingly Meffengers were fent to attend him with it, but the Army fruftrated all thofe endeavours.

156. Some other things were pafs'd that day, and left the Parliament fhould be wanting to it felf in doing what was poffible for its defence and the Citys, in cafe the Army fhould not ftop upon their Letter, the Committee of Safety is reviv'd, and order'd, as before, to join with the
Mi-

Militia, and provide for their protection; and all but need, for Sir *Thomas Fairfax* and his two Councils of War, the Members and the Officers, would not vouchsafe to read the Letter, but march on *Rabshekah* like, threatning ruin and destruction; yet was there no such thought towards them, our End being not *vim inferre*, but *repellere*, get such a strength about us as might only defend, not offend. To that end those Forces which were quarter'd further off in *Kent* and *Surrey*, as Sir *Robert Pye*'s Company, Colonel *Graves's*, and some others, were commanded to draw near the City, not offering or intending any act of hostility, when upon a sudden, the Sunday morning the 2d of *August*, a Party of Horse, about two Regiments, commanded, as I take it, by one *Desborough* a Major, fell into *Deptford*, where were some half a score of Sir *Robert Pye*'s Soldiers who had staid behind the rest to discharge the Quarters, and most inhumanly and basely butcher'd those poor Men as many as they could light of, killing besides any that look'd like a Soldier whom they found upon the way, some within a stones cast of the works of *Southwark*. This, as it was a most barbarous and bloody Murder (which will bring down vengeance up-

upon their heads foon or late, that tho they fhould efcape the hand of Juftice here, the hand of God will certainly overtake them) fo did it fomething awaken the City to fee their own danger, and a little quicken their pace to draw the Ordnance upon their Works, and man them fomething better ; but in truth not much. For I may fay they were a people prepar'd for ruin and flavery, *Gibbs* and *Fowks* principally had bewitch'd them ; and Agents for the Army who were up and down, weaken'd Mens hearts and hands, fo as nothing was done to any purpofe for putting them into a way of fafety, or poffibility of deliverance. All were defirous equally of Peace, but not all equally afraid of Danger ; thofe who fear'd it moft were the greateft caufe of it : and fome good well meaning Men of the Affembly, Mr. *Herbert Palmer* and others, whom Mr. *Marfbal* had wrought upon and perfwaded to come to the Houfes firft, as being Minifters and Ambaffadors of Peace, to perfwade to Peace, and then to the Common Council to do the like to them; which did but difhearten and difcourage thofe who were apt enough to fear, being not fo fully ready to refift a power that was coming upon them, and did hinder the preparations. To fay the truth,

truth all was done that could be to hinder and little to help. Infomuch as at that very time when the Army was marching up for their deſtruction, about 49000 *l.* which had formerly been order'd to be ſent down for the Army's drawing off further from the City, could not be privily convey'd out of Town by Sir *John Wollaſton,* and ſome others, in which. Mr. *Scawen* and Mr. *Allen* Members of the Houſe, had a principal hand, which was as great a blow to Parliament and City as could be given ; for it ſerv'd to keep the Soldiers together, and unite them for marching up, whereas before there were high diſcontents amongſt them, and it weaken'd us, even taking away ſo much of our blood, that which at that time we principally ſtood in need of.

157. The Parliament did all that could be deſir'd, yet ſtill with a reſolution to endeavour the ways of preventing extremities. Thoſe Commiſſioners of theirs who were at the Army had in a manner diſavowed them, for never any thing came from them to the Houſes ; and Mr. *Skippon,* when the City ſent to him to come and take the conduct and management

M

ment of their bufinefs, a duty they might very well have expeɛed from him, he was fo far from performing it as he abfolutely refus'd except he might have an affurance from the Parliament, and from them, to return again to the Army if he lik'd not his conditions, which was a great ingratitude to thofe who had deferv'd fo well of him, and an unworthy complyance with them who had formerly negleɛed him.

158. A Meffage was refolv'd upon to be fent to the Army, to fee if they could be ftopp'd from coming in that manner to endanger putting all into blood; Mr. *Swifen* and Mr. *Afhurft* as I remember were nominated, the reft I have forgot. The like was alfo prepar'd in the City, and more quickly executed; upon Tuefday Alderman *Gibbs*, Mr. *Noel*, and fome other Aldermen and Common Councilmen were appointed to go with it. And they foon return'd, not with an Olive branch, but with a heavy doom to the honour of the City, freedom of the Parliament, and fafety of the poor eleven Members in the firft place, and next of all that had engag'd in the defence of the City. The Keys of the City (if I

mifmisremember not) muſt be deliver'd to his Excellency, all the Works from the *Thames* ſide to *Iſlington* Fort demoliſht, the eleven Members ſecur'd or given up, and all the Reformados and Officers like-wiſe who were ready to have fought for them. This was as worthily by the Common Council yielded to, their Am-baſſadors notably promoting it. The e-leven Members were not yet ſeiz'd nor deliver'd, but as bad, left to ſhift for themſelves, no care at all taken for their preſervation, tho the City had now this laſt time wholly embark'd in their trou-ble, and engag'd them in their buſineſs, petitioning the Houſe of Commons to enjoin them to attend the Service of the Houſe, themſelves not at all moving in, or deſiring it: Nay, they did not ſo much as provide for Major General *Maſſey,* whom they had made their Commander in chief; but like *Iſachar* bow'd under the Burden, betray'd themſelves and all that had to do with them.

159. Here was an end of the Parlia-ment, and in truth of the City, all whoſe Glory is laid in the duſt; and as it was high before in reputation both at home and abroad, ſo is it now be-

come

come a hiffing and reproach to all that fee it or hear of it. The next day Sir *Thomas Fairfax* fends to take poffeffion, and the day after that matches in ftate, bringing with him thofe deferting Lords and Commons, and the Earl of *Manche-ſter* and Mr. *Lenthal,* the two pretended Speakers, not vouchſafing to look upon the Lord Mayor and Aldermen, who were there with the Recorder, provided with a Speech for his entertainment, which he did not ſo well deferve, as they did that ſcorn then put upon them.

160. He goes ſtrait to the Houſes, put thofe two Men in the Speakers pla-ces, who had no more right to them than himſelf, and has ever ſince con-tinu'd them there by force, and keep-ing out the true Speakers ; which the Lord *Willoughby* is to the Peers (that Houfe being under an adjournment, and not ſitting when the Intruder came in, ſo not in a capacity to admit him) and Mr. *Pelham* to the Commons, who had been legally chofen when the Houſe was free and under no force ; the other ha-ving deferted, which is of all Crimes the greateſt.

161. So as without him it is no Houfe, but an Affembly of Men acting under the Army without lawful authority; fome of them by a combination and agreement with the Army, but far the greater part by a terror and an awe from it, and therefore to be look'd upon accordingly ; and queftionlefs many of them continuing there out of a good intent, like fo many *Hufbais*, only to defeat the pernicious Counfels of thofe *Achitophels* who had defign'd the deftruction of *David*, the ruin of honeft Men, and even the trouble and confufion of the whole *Ifrael* of God, Church and State. Thefe are fo far from deferving thereby either to become the object of blame or pardon, as they merit exceedingly, are worthy the praife both of prefent and future times ; but to be confider'd rather as faithful Patriots, that act out of neceffity in an extraordinary way, ftand in the Gap to keep off mifchief, than as Members of Parliament able or indeed qualify'd to exercife any parliamentary Power for the good of the Kingdom ; the Houfe having been difturb'd, and for the time fupprefs'd by a real Force, not feign'd and imaginary as the other was ; and while this force continues,

M 3

tinues, not fuffer'd to come together, but as foon as it ceafes will return of it felf to be as it was before.

162. For there is a difference between thefe two Cafes, one the Parliaments act-ing under a force, remaining ftill to be a Parliament, which dos not annul it, nor the Acts it dos; but makes them fit to be repeal'd, yet ftanding good *pro tempore*.

163. Many of our beft Laws have been fo made (when Armies have been on foot) and afterwards declar'd good in a free Parliament; and what then done did appear to be inconvenient and unjuft, was by fubfequent Parliaments re-peal'd. So is it fit that what was compel'd to be done by the Apprentices and others in that tumultuous way, the Monday that the force was, fhould be repeal'd, as not fit to be continu'd. And fo all that has been done a great while, under the power and force of the Army, fince it firft rebel'd and gave Laws to the Parliament, is as fit, if not more, to be hereafter re-peal'd; and queftionlefs will, if ever the Parliament come to be free again. Nay, even thefe pretenders do us that right,

as

as finding the proceedings of the Parliament after their defertion not futable to their Ends, but againft them, by an Ordinance to repeal and declare them null; which otherwife had not been needful, feeing they would fall of themfelves, being Crimes in their own nature as proceeding from an ufurp'd Authority. This is one cafe; the other is, when a force proceeds fo far and fo high as not to fuffer a Parliament to be, gives it fuch a wound as for the time it cannot act, but muft ceafe, even as a wounded Body that lies in a Trance without fenfe or motion: But when that force is over, and the Spirits recollected, it returns to it felf to do the functions of life, move and act asformerly. It is but like a Parenthefis in a Sentence, and remains one and the fame as if the Parenthefis were not at all.

164. But to return where I left. This General, a fetter up and puller down of Parliaments, has a Chair fet him in either Houfe, where firft in the Lords Houfe, then in the Commons, thofe pretended Speakers make Speeches to him, giving him thanks for all, approving his Declaration of the Reafons of his coming

M 4   to

to *London*, defiring him to go on in taking care for the fecurity of the Kingdom, and to appoint a Guard for the. Parliament. Than which there was never any thing more bafe ; but Mr. *Lenthal* exceeded, being both bafe and prophane, applying a *Higgaior Selah.* to this laft act of his Excellency, who as wifely took it. Then that the prophanefs might be compleat, and God mock'd as well as Men abus'd, they appoint the Thurfday after for a day of Thankfgiving, and fitted it with Preachers, Mr. *Marfhal* and Mr. *Nye*, *Simeon* and *Levi*, where they fay *Marfhal* outwent all that had gone before him, and his Brother *Nye* was a modeft Presbyterian in comparifon of him; but that Apoftate went beyond *Ela*, making this deliverance a greater one than the Gunpowder Treafon, as I have been credibly inform'd by thofe that heard him. And fome few days after, Sir *Thomas Fairfax* and the whole Army marcht in triumph with Lawrel in their Hats as Conquerors, through the fubdu'd City of *London*, to fhew it was at his mercy ; which was an airy vanity I confefs above my underftanding, and might have rais'd a fpirit of Indignation, not fo eafily to have been laid. But a higher infolency

of

of an Army compos'd of fo mean people, and a more patient humble fubmiffion and bearing of a great and popu-
lous City, but a little before fo full of
honour and greatnefs, was, I think, never heard of.

165. And now the Houfes fall to voting, the Lords leading the way, and
outdoing the Commons, as much as Mr.
Lenthal outdid the Earl of *Manchefter* in
the Thankfgiving, or Mr. *Marfhal* did
Mr. *Nye* in the thankfgiving Sermon.
They make Sir *Thomas Fairfax* Genera-
liffimo, Commander in chief of all the
Forces in the Kingdom, and Conftable of
the Tower, otherwife fignifying Mr. *O-
liver Cromwel*, of whom Sir *Thomas* was the
fhadow ; they thank his Excellency over
again for his care of the fafety of the
City and Parliament, *Rifum teneatis a-
mici* ; leave it wholly to him to appoint
what Guards he thinks fit for their fecurity, *Sed quis cuftodiet cuftodes ?* give a
months Pay for a gratuity to the Army
for their many good Services, which is
præmium nequitiæ ; then fet up the Star
Chamber, the High Commiffion, the Spanifh Inquifition, in one Committee of ten
Lords and twenty Commoners (read o-
ver but their names, and you will fwear
it,

it, except for four of the Commoners, who are very unequally yok'd, sixteen againſt them) to ſit in the painted Chamber *de die in diem*, to examine the buſineſs of the Mutiny, and of forcing the Houſes.

166. So far the Lords lead and the Commons follow; but in another Vote they go by themſelves a good while, that all things done by the Members ſince (as they injuriouſly and falſly pretend) the Speakers and other Members were driven away from the Parliament, be annull'd, and of no effect, and declar'd to have been ſo at the making thereof. The Commons can't agree to this, but put off the debate to another time. Some ſenſe of honour there was amongſt them, and of the dangerous conſequence of ſuch a Vote, beſides the unreaſonableneſs and injuſtice, taking away the Authority by which thoſe Votes were made, and ſo expoſing to queſtion and ruin all ſuch as were at the paſſing of them, or had acted by them. Many days debates were ſpent upon it, but it could not be carry'd, the Houſe of Commons would be a Houſe of Commons ſtill; and as they repreſent the people of *England*, ſo aſſert their Liberties, if they were left to themſelves, and not overaw'd by the power of the Army.   167.

167. Therefore the Agitators muſt to work again with an humble Addreſs to his Excellency, and ſome Propoſals on behalf of the Kingdom and the Army: Firſt, That all thoſe that have ſat at *Weſtminſter*, uſurping a parliamentary Authority, ſince the forcible expulſion of the Parliament, may immediately be excluded the Houſe. Secondly, That thoſe Members who have adher'd to that pretended Parliament, may be alſo excluded under a penalty if they preſume to ſit. Thirdly, That all former Votes againſt diſaffected Members may be put in execution. And this is to make a free Parliament, for thoſe Rogues to determine who ſhall ſit, who ſhall not, and how they ſhall be puniſh'd who diſobey them. Theſe Lords and Commoners deſerve well of Parliament and Kingdom, that ran away from the Parliament, and went to the Army for this.

168. Sir *Thomas Fairfax* and the Council of War anſwer preſently, for it is but a Song of two parts, making one harmony, all ſet by the ſame hand. A Remonſtrance is forthwith produc'd and ſent to both Houſes the 18*th* of *Auguſt*,

a

a forrowful Ditty for the poor Houfe of
Commons, which tells them plainly, after a long deduction of all paffages,
juft lying over the fame Lies again,
That thofe Members which fat during the
abfence of the Speakers, are guilty of the
profecution and maintenance of the faid
treafonable engagement and violence, and
therefore muft not be their Judges (but
their adverfe Party fhall be theirs, which
is Army Juftice) That they might have
been made Prifoners of War ; wherefore
they proteft and declare, if they hereafter intrude themfelves to fit in Parliament, they can no longer fuffer it, but
will take fome fpeedy effectual courfe,
that both they and others guilty of the
fame practices may be brought to con-
dign punifhment.

169. And they back this Remonftrance
(for which the Lords return a Letter of
approbation and great thanks to his Excellency for his continu'd care of the honour and freedom of Parliament) with a
Party of a thoufand Horfe drawn up to
Hide-Park; *Cromwel* and *Ireton* making
menacing Speeches in the Houfe, and
Guards out of the Army befetting the
doors and avenues. By all which means,
and

and the terror of their furly impeaching looks. (as fome of the Pamphleteers obferve it) many of the Members were driven away, and the poor Houfe forc'd the 20th of *Auguft*, to pafs the Ordinance for declaring all Votes, Orders, and Ordinances, made in one or both Houfes from *July* 26 till *Auguft* 6, null and void. And now they are a free Parliament, or as *Haflerig* told them the next day after the eleven Members were withdrawn, a glorious Parliament, in truth no Parliament, but they are what Mr. *Cromwel* will have them to be.

170. Then they lay about them, impeach feven Lords of High Treafon, fparing only my Lord of *Pembrook*. They proceed againft fome of their own Members, fufpend Mr. *Bainton*, put Commiffary *Copley* and Mr. Recorder out of the Houfe, whom they commit to the Tower for high Mifdemeanours, expel likewife Sir *John Maynard*, and fend him to the Tower. The reft of the eleven Members upon the City's delivering up it felf and the Parliament to the will of the Army, having fent for their Paffes which the Houfe had order'd, and upon them withdrawn themfelves into foreign

reign parts, the Lord Mayor and some
of the Aldermen were likewise imprison'd
in the Tower, and charg'd with Treason : And all honest Men persecuted,
threaten'd, and therefore fled and scat-
ter'd, some one way and some another ;
and these are the effects of a free Parliament.

171. The Lieutenant of the Tower,
Colonel *West*, an honest and gallant Man,
after he had been at charge to treat and
entertain Sir *Thomas Fairfax*, coming to
take possession of his Place as Constable,
was by that worthy General, by way
of thankfulness for his good entertainment, turn'd out : And an Independent,
one *Tichburn* a Linen Draper , put in,
which was done with so much insolency and scorn of the City, as when his
favourite Alderman *Gibbs* had prepar'd
a long winded Speech in the name of the
City, who crav'd it as a Boon and Act
of Grace, that he would keep in the old
Lieutenant, he cut him off short, and bid
him speak no more of it. Indeed it had
been against his Instructions, and the
Maxim of his Master *Cromwel* and all
that faction, which is to suffer none in any
power save such as are theirs Body and
Soul, and put all others out.   172.

172. So Colonel *Pointz* was feiz'd upon, and by force fetch'd out of his Command in the North ; Major General *Maffey* muſt not continue in his of the Weſt ;
Captain *Patten* turn'd out of his Vice
Admiralſhip, and *Rainsborough* put in ;
Colonel *Carne* out of the Government of
the Iſle of *Wight*, and *Hammond* in his
room.   The Self-denying Ordinance was
a trick for this purpoſe.   In the begin-
ing of theſe troubles Sir *William Lewis*
not agreeing with their Palate, being Go-
vernour of *Portſmouth*, they make the
Earl of *Eſſex*, who was then General,
ſend for him, upon a ſuppoſition that he
was a favourer of Malignants, and of many other things ; which being examin'd
by the Committee of Safety, he gave ſo
good an account of himſelf, as the Committee could not do leſs than write a
Letter in his juſtification to the General, leaving it to him to repair him as
he thought fit.   Then ſome of theſe honeſt
Men, who themſelves had ſubſcrib'd to
it, ſent a Letter privately to my Lord
of *Eſſex*, by which they advis'd his not
ſending him back to *Portſmouth* ; which
jugling of theirs he receiv'd with indignation, and wiſh'd Sir *William Lewis* to
re-

return to his Command: but he feeing
what Men he had to deal with, quitted
the Employment; and to fay the truth,
he only can be happy who has nothing
to do with them, except it be in punifh-
ing them according to their demerits.

173. They have now they think both
Houfes to their minds, ready to do whatfoever they pleafe. Accordingly the Houfe
of Commons orders thofe of the eleven
Members, who were beyond Sea upon their
Paffes, which gave them liberty of travelling fix Months, to appear the 16*th* of
October, taking no courfe to have them
fummon'd, only notice to be given at
their Houfes, or places of their laft abode,
where few of us had any Servants, my
felf only an old Porter and a Maid or
two.

174. Then they go on to the publick
bufinefs, fuch work as the Army had cut
out for them. Which were certain Propofals that Sir *Thomas Fairfax* and the
Council of War had fent them the 1*st* of
Auguft, fign'd by *John Rufhworth* Secretary, now far above *John Brown* and *Hen-*
ry Elfing. In thefe they fet down a new
platform of Government, an *Utopia* of
their

their own, take upon them to alter all,
give Rules to all, cajole the King, claw
with the people, cheat both, never intending good to either.   The reading of the
Articles themselves which are in print
will satisfie every body ; they need no
Comment, and are so many, and of so
vast a comprehension, as to treat of them
all, to shew the absurdities, contradictions,
impossibilities, unreasonableness, which
many of them contain, would swell this
to too big a Volume. I will only speak to
some few, and shew how they dissolve the
whole frame of this Monarchy, taking a
sunder every part, pulling out every pin
and new making it. First, The constitu-
tions and proceedings of Parliaments, pro-
jecting new things for their beginnings,
continuances, and endings, for the elections of Members, privileges and customs
of the Houses, which they had violated
before *de facto*, but now must be alter'd
de jure.   The Militia of the Kingdom,
where they will have a General appointed
to command it, Pay setled to maintain it,
a Council of State to superintend it, which
signifies to establish by Act of Parliament
this holy Army, the Council of War, and
General *Cromwel*. Then matters of the
Church, where they will have no power

exercis'd to preferve Religion and Piety; they would have Bifhops fo they may be juft Cyphers, and all Acts to be repeal'd, which hinder Men from being Atheifts or Independents; for no body muft be enjoyn'd to come to the Church, and there may be Meetings to practife any thing of fuperftition and folly, the Covenant muft be laid afide. In fum, it is to take away all Government and fet up Independency. They propofe a new way for making grand Jury-men, Juftices of Peace, and Sheriffs. When thefe and many other things which they mention are fettled, which will take up time enough, then the King, Queen, and Royal Iffue to be reftor'd, which is as much as juft nothing. Next they make the people believe they do as great matters for them, will have a liberty of petitioning, which is but to make way for fchifmatical feditious Petitions; for if any Petition ftick at their *Diana,* none fo fierce to punifh. Who more than they againft all the Petitions from *London* and the Counties for disbanding of the Army, and complaining of their factious ways? how eager were they againft the Petitions promoted in the City in the beginning, for which *Benion* was fined, and many troubled; and forne Petitions out of *Kent,* for which

which some Gentlemen were committed ?
How barbarously did they fall upon some
poor women which came one time to *Westminster* petitioning for Peace, commanding a Troop of Horse to run over them,
the Train'd Bands to shoot at them, whereby many were wounded and some kill'd ?
Yet the world must think they will have
it free for all to petition. Then they will
have the Excise taken off from some Com-
modities whereon the poor people live,
and a time limited for taking off the
whole; which was but to please and amuse
them till they had got the mastery of those
who they thought stood in their way : but
being Masters themselves, they soon sent
out a Command (more now than any Pro-
clamation or Ordinance) to forbid all Soldiers any way to interrupt the levying
of the Excise, or any other Tax charg'd
by the Parliament, which they had made
merely instrumental to poll the people for
the support of them and their Faction.
They will have no Tythes to be paid,
and so Ministers to be starv'd, for in truth
they would have no Ministers at all, or rather no Ministery ; like *Julian* the Apo-
state, take away *presbyterium* not *presbyte-
ros* : for Ministers that will be subservient
to them, like Mr. *Marshal,* shall be much

made

made of. The rules and courfe of Law muft be reduc'd; indeed they will need no Law, for they will rule by the Sword, and the Councils of War fhall fupply all Courts of Juftice. Prifoners for debt, if they have not wherewith to pay, muft be freed; fo we may be fure few debts fhall be fatisfy'd, for it is an eafie thing fo to convey or conceal an Eftate, as nothing vifible will be left for doing right to Creditors. None muft be compell'd to anfwer to queftions tending to the accufing themfelves or their neareft Relations in criminal Caufes, witnefs their Orders to make men under great Penalties ftate their Cafe in no lefs matter than Treafon; therefore this is underftood to extend only to the privilege of their own Faction. We muft alter all Statutes and Cuftoms of Corporations, and of impofing Oaths which may be conftru'd to the moleftation of religious people, that is, Independents, for all others are Greeks and Barbarians. Yet thefe men, in how many Letters and Declarations do they fay and proteft, they have no thought of fetting up Independency, nor to meddle with any thing but what concerns the Soldiery, and leave all the reft to the wifdom of the Parliament. Indeed they conclude their Propofals with what concerns

cerns the Soldiery : That provifion may be made for payment of Arrears to the Army, and the reft of the Soldiers of the Kingdom who have concurr'd with them in their late proceedings : and in the next place, of the publick debts and damages of the Kingdom, which they have taken a courfe that the Parliament fhall never fatisfie, having caus'd fuch a debt to the Soldiers, and fo infupportable a charge for the maintenance of the Army, which is to be fatisfy'd in the firft place before other debts to the reft of the Kingdom, that the Subject is not able to bear it, but is utterly ruin'd.

175. To fome of thefe Heads they fay they will offer fome fpeedy particulars in the nature of Rules, of good ufe to the publick : Rules indeed, from which, and from the Rulers, good Lord deliver us. But here you fee they compile a work like the fecond part of *Solomon*'s, treating from the Cedar in *Lebanon* to the Hyfop on the Wall; of all degrees and conditions, from the King that fhould be on the Throne to the Beggar in Prifon. And fince they have brought both ends together, fo now we have a free Parliament and a free Kingdom.

176.

176. Every day produces some effects
of their tyranny and power, like another
Africk, some Monster, tho they were not
without their difficulties to wreftle with
and overcome. For to bring fo abfolute a
Bondage upon a people that was free before, could not be without many heats
and colds. They had the King to deal
with, whom they muft in fome meafure
fatisfie and perfwade that they had good
intentions for him, to reftore and maintain him in a power and dignity futable
to his Royal Perfon and Office, from which
the truth and bottom of their defign did
differ *toto cælo* : they had the King's Party,
whom they muft entertain in hopes and
expectation, and then cozen ; they had
the Parliament which muft be kept under,
brought to obedience, and a total fubfer-
vience to their will and command. They
had the generality of the people, who were
for Government and Monarchy founded
upon Peace (as they had reafon) defirous
to be eas'd of their Burdens and Taxes,
with hopes whereof the Army had fed
them, but it ftood not with their Intereft
to procure it them. They had laftly their
own faction which troubled them moft of
all, being violent, impatient, not to be
gain'd

gain'd to go the pace of their Grandees, and wait the revolutions of time, which they defir'd might have taken place, for the fame things to be effected which even thofe headftrong furious people coveted, but with more eafe, advantage, and great-nefs to themfelves.

177. For they apprehended it very dangerous to fall prefently upon his Maje-fty and break with him, feeing the in-clinations of the people towards him, and he at liberty for all perfons to have accefs unto him, whom he might confer with, inform, and difpofe according to occafion, perhaps take fome refolutions which they apprehended might turn to their preju-dice. Befides, they knew not how the Scotifh Nation might then declare and engage, which with the help of thofe whom they had already difcontented by their injuftice and oppreffion in the execu-tion of their particular malice and revenge, and thofe whom they fhould difcontent by fruftrating their expectation, having born them in hand with hopes of Peace and freedom from Taxes, muft needs have given a great interruption to their proceed-ings, and even fhake the foundation of their whole defign; therefore they muft

work

work in another way, make his Majefty believe they will do great things for
him, fo to receive rather an advantage
than hinderance from his influence upon
the affections of the Kingdom. To this
end were all thofe applications to him by
Cromwel, Ireton, and the reft of their Creatures and Inftruments, in framing of the
propofals, appearing for his intereft in the
Houfe, feeming to defire his reftitution,
being now turn'd abfolute Courtiers. They
knew it would at laft come all to one
with that which they have fince done to
him. For, coming to a fettlement with
his concurrence, they had the power, he but
vanam imaginem ; and what of luftre and
quietnefs had been contributed by his Majefty's conjunction, would but have ferv'd
to have confirm'd and heighten'd their
authority, all had been but Stilts to raife
them above the reft of the Kingdom and
himfelf likewife ; fo as it had been in their
power (as well as we are fure it had been
in their will) to deftroy him afterwards,
he fhould have only been a little longer
repriev'd, as *Ulyffes* was by *Polyphemus* to
be devour'd at laft.

178. But the Party would not give way
to this ; hatred to the King, envy and jealoufies

*

loufies againft their afpiring Leaders, and a violent defire of having the work done at once, lay all perfons and things level on the fudden, bring forth their monftrous conceptions all at one birth, made them break out, flye in their faces, difcover many of their villanies, and, as appears by that bufinefs of *Lilburn* and *Wildman*, even refolve to take *Cromwel* out of the way, and murder him for an Apoftate.

179. When *Cromwel, Ireton,* and the reft faw this, and that this madnefs of the inferiour fort of their Difciples, which had formerly rais'd them, fupported them, and lately given them the advantage of their Enemies, victory over the Parliament, and a fuperiority over all the Kingdom, would now be their ruin, if either they clos'd throughly with the King (for then their Party would forfake them, turn againft them, and they knew they had fo well merited of King and Kingdom, as not to expect to be preferv'd in greatnefs, either for honefty or abilities) or if the King continu'd at liberty at *Hampton-Court,* or any other place, where freedom of refort might be to him, and opportunities taken and improv'd to meet with and

pre-

prevent all their attempts, that then it would be impossible to carry on their business in an open and declar'd way of violence against him.   They saw a necessity of removing him, and making sure his person ; that done, they thought they might be bold to do and say what they would, and own a second time the actings and resolutions of the Agitators.

180. The difficulty was how to bring this about, to cozen the King so as to make him act it himself, and flie into the Cage ; carry him by force they durst not, it would be unhandsom, it might be dangerous : They use this stratagem, heighten and sharpen underhand the mad humour of their Party against him, to have it break out all manner of ways, in threatning Speeches, Pamphlets ; some consultations that whilst his Majesty liv'd in *England* he could not be safe ; meetings to consider and come to some resolutions of taking him out of the way : the Army is again disquiet, the Officers not obey'd, all things tending to mutiny, and some violent eruption.   Then dos Mr. *Cromwel* and his Cabinet Council seem to be extreamly solicitous of the safety of his Majesty's person, cause some discoveries to be
given

given him of his danger, expreſs great indignation and trouble in the Houſe, in the Army, and other places againſt theſe proceedings, act their parts ſo to the life, as the Life of a Man muſt go to make up the diſguiſe: an Agitator whom at a Council of War, with two more, they condemned, was ſhot to death; ſo as the King could not but have a great confidence in theſe Men to believe that they were really for his preſervation. At laſt *Cromwel* writes a Letter to *Whalley* (who commands the Guards about his Majeſty's Perſon) to be ſhewn his Majeſty; and other informations are likewiſe brought him, to make him believe that if he eſcap'd not preſently he will be murder'd; and he is advis'd to go to the Iſle of *Wight*, where they had beforehand provided him a Jaylor, Colonel *Hammond*, one for whom they ſaid they could anſwer, that there his Majeſty would be in ſafety, and they able to ſerve him.

181. Here they have the King ſafe enough, and now the Army is preſently quiet, the Agitators as obedient as Lambs, and Councils of War are ſet up again to act as formerly. And Sir *Thomas Fairfax*, with their advice, ſets out a Remonſtrance

ftrance to give fatisfaction to the Army,
which he concludes with a Proteftation,
to adhere to, conduct, live and die with
the Army in the profecution of fome things
there exprefs'd ; as namely, To obtain a
prefent provifion for conftant Pay, ftating
of Accounts, fecurity for Arrears, with
an effectual and fpeedy courfe to raife
Monies, a period to be fet to this Parliament, provifion for future Parliaments,
the certainty of their meeting, fitting, and
ending, the freedom and equality of E-
lections, and other things which he had
the impudence and boldnefs to publifh in
print.

182. And now inftead of the Propofals,
they intend to fend the four Bills to his
Majefty to fign, which done, they would
treat with him. By thefe Bills the Army
was to be eftablifh'd, which was the Englifh of that for the Militia ; and by another of them they would make fure, that
the countenance of the Parliament and the
acting of the Army fhould never be fepa-
rated ; which was the intent of that for
power of adjourning. So as if at any time
the juft fenfe of Indignation, of fo many
Indignities and Injuries offer'd by the Army to all ranks of Men, Magiftrates both
fu-

fupreme and fubordinate, people of all conditions and degrees fhould ftir them up to fome endeavours of cafting off this iron Yoke; their Party in Parliament, with their Speaker Mr. *Lenthal*'s help, fhould prefently be ready to adjourn to the Army, then damn and deftroy all the world by colour of Law and power of the Sword; fo King and Kingdom muft be fubject to a perpetual flavery by Act of Parliament.

183. The Scots were laid afide in this Addrefs to his Majefty, contrary to the Treaty, and contrary to the Covenant. By the Treaty there ought to have been no application for Peace but with their advice and confent; here the Scots did not only not advife nor confent, but proteft againft it. By the Covenant all were bound to keep united, firm and clofe one to another, not to fuffer themfelves to be divided; here thefe Men do divide from the whole Kingdom of *Scotland*, make a rent and breach between the Kingdoms in fettling of the Peace, the very end both of Treaty and Covenant.

184. And for that fubterfuge, that it is againft the privilege of Parliament that
any

any out of the Houses should interpose, or have any thing to do with Bills, it is a mere cavil, Fig-leaves which cover not their nakedness ; for that would have been no more against Privilege, than was the whole transaction of business in carrying on of the War, and managing other great concernments of Parliament and Kingdom, wherein the Scots all along were admitted to participate in Counsel and Interest.

185. The King refusing to sign these Bills, *Hammond,* by Sir *Thomas Fairfax's* single order, claps him up a Prisoner, removes all his Servants. It seems by this time they had forgot their Remonstrance of the 23*d* of *June,* where they say it is against their principles to imprison the King, and that there can be no Peace without due consideration of his Majesty's Rights : But then was then, and now is now. It was then necessary for the good of their Affairs to seem gracious, desirous of Peace, and of restoring the King. Now they appear in their own colours, their nature having no restraint ; nay, Sir *Thomas Fairfax's* Command is so absolute and sacred, as Captain *Burley* was hang'd for endeavouring

to

to oppose it, there being at that time no other pretence for his Majesty's Imprisonment, but because Sir *Thomas Fairfax* had commanded it : it is true, that upon his signification to the Houses of what he had done, it was approv'd of and confirm'd.

186. All this while a rigorous hand is continu'd against the impeach'd Lords who were under the Black Rod, the Gentlemen of the House of Commons, the Lord Mayor and Aldermen in the Tower, who had been kept Prisoners so many Months, upon a general Impeachment, and no particular Charge against them. It was often endeavour'd in the House to have pass'd the Articles which were brought in against the Lord *Willoughby*, to be a leading Case to the rest. Where I cannot pass by, that I find he is charg'd with Treason for levying War against the King, and this done by the same persons that imprison the King, and had hang'd *Burley* for levying War for him : One may see they will find matter to hang on all hands. Many debates were had on this business, and at last it was resolv'd to lay the Articles aside.

187. The seven Lords still press'd for
their

their Trial, the Houfe of Peers as often fent down to the Houfe of Commons to give them notice of it ; and no Charge coming up, they fet them at liberty. The Common Council likewife petition'd for the liberty of their Members in the Tower ; which the Army took fo heinoufly, as that and the laying afide of the Charge againft the Lord *Willoughby*, together with a Vote which had pafs'd for disbanding the fupernumerary Forces, produce a thundring Remonftrance of *December* the 7*th*, cafting in the Parliaments teeth their delays and neglects : That the Army had with patience waited four Months upon them : That finding fuch obftructions in matters of fupply, and fuch unworthy requital, they apprehended God upbraids their care to preferve a people given up to their own deftruction : That they could, to fpeak Amen, with the power and advantages God had put into their hands (for fo is their expreffion) have put the Army and other Forces engag'd with it into fuch a pofture as to have affur'd themfelves of Pay, and made their oppofers have follow'd them with offers of fatisfaction : That now all bufinefs feems to be wrapt up in one bare Vote, That all fupernumery Forces fhould

be

be disbanded, which Vote they fay they cannot imagine to be abfolute and fove-raign : They offer as their final advice, that 40000 *l.* more *per menfem* be added to the 60000 *l.* that is in all 100000 *l.* a Month. That for the more fure and rea-dy payment, the Forces may be imme-diately affign'd to feveral Counties, out of whofe Taxes they fhall be paid, and the General have power to make thofe diftributions. And many things more they offer, or rather order for the pay-ment of the Soldiers fo peremptorily, as if it be not granted and pafs'd effectually by the end of that prefent week, they fay they can give no longer account of the Army in a regular way ; but if they find not fatisfaction in their judgments, muft take fome extraordinary ways of power. Then they come and vent their malice againft the City, of which they fay they have been fo tender ; witnefs their carriage in their late advance to-wards it, notwithftanding provocations, their innocent march through it, their patient waiting for their long due Ar-rears. But now Juftice forces them to defire that (the adjacent Counties being undone, and the whole Kingdom groan-ing under the oppreffions of free Quarter,

O whilft

whilſt the City, which occaſions all, is
free of it) there be no longer ſtop to the
drawing thither of the Army : That beſides levying the arrear of the Tax, it
make reparation to the parts adjacent of
100000 *l.* damage : That if they be ne-
ceſſitated or call'd on by the County, they
muſt on their behalf demand of the City
to the full : They earneſtly deſire that the
proceedings againſt the Citizens and o-
thers impeach'd may be haſten'd, and that
out of their Fines and Confiſcations ſome
part of reparation be made to the Country. Then they ſay they ſee not how the
Parliament can ſit in ſafety if the Army
ſhould never ſo little withdraw, when
they find the Common Council, thro the
Parliament and Army's lenity, take the
boldneſs already, in the face of both, to
intercede for the releaſe and acquittal, or
rather juſtification of thoſe impeach'd Perſons, who are but fellow Delinquents to
moſt of that Council : That the conſideration of this, and the renew'd confidence
of Mr. *Gwin,* and other Members, partakers in the ſame things, who preſume
to ſit in the Houſe, makes them fear, that
through lenity and moderation, ſo much of
the ſame Leven is left behind, as even the
worſt of the eleven Members (notwithſtanding

ftanding their double Crimes) may be again call'd for in, unleſs the Houſe by ſome excluſive reſolutions and proceedings do timely prevent the ſame.

188. Indeed theſe are gracious Princes, full of lenity and moderation, by their own ſayings; but they dwell by ill Neighbours, that they muſt commend themſelves, for no body elſe will do it. The Parliament is beholden to them, they tell them their faults, bid them not truſt ſo much to their Votes, which are not abſolute nor ſoveraign; let them know what is their duty to do, and give a ſhort day to perform it in, left they ſhould be idle, and a worſe thing fall upon them. The Country is beholden to them, who now know the worſt of it; 100000 *l.* to be monthly rais'd to eaſe them of Taxes, and the Exciſe according to promiſe: but then they have to help them, reparation from the City for former damages, and the perſons appointed out of whoſe Eſtates it muſt be paid by way of Fine or Confiſcation, whether they prove guilty or no; and they are not wanting in their expreſſions to the City of their tenderneſs of it, wherefore they give good inſtance, coming againſt it with Banners diſplay'd,

O 2　　　　　Horſe

Horfe and Foot armed, Cannon loaden, and only take poffeffion of their Works and of the Tower, change their Militia, take from them *Weftminfter* and *South-wark*, commit their Mayor and principal Aldermen, yet doing the City no hurt (like the Fryer in *Chaucer*, who would have but of the Capon the Liver, and of a Pig the head, yet nothing for him fhould be dead) then marching through it fo innocently, only putting that fcorn upon them which none of their Kings ever did when moft provok'd ; that to have en-dur'd a plundering had been more honou-rable : Then waited fo patiently for their Arrears, when they had a great part of the 200000 *l.* which the City had lent for their disbanding, had taken that Mo-ney, yet would not disband, and deftroy'd Trade by their late Rebellion ; and now having fo long lain upon free quarter all about , that they had made Provifions exceffive dear, and almoft famifh'd the City, to exprefs a defire to come and quarter in it, which fure was for their good, only Juftice made them move they fhould pay 100000 *l.* for reparation to the Country; that their beft Members, greateft Aldermen, and others, and their Lord Mayor, whom they had caus'd to

be

be unjuftly committed, fhould be as unjuftly fin'd and ruin'd; and then charge
fo honourable a Court as the Common
Council with Treafon.

189. Then for the eleven Members,
how much they are beholden to them is
beyond expreffion, all their Remonftrances, as well as this make it appear; here
they defir'd only they might have a Writ
of eafe from attending the Parliament a-
ny more, out of their abounding care
for the freedom of Parliaments, and the
free fitting and voting of the Members.

190. And they will be fure to have
all put in execution, the refractory
Houfe of Commons fhall make them wait
no longer. A Regiment or two of Foot
march and quarter in *White-Hall*, as many Horfe in the *Mews* (they having provided another Lodging for the King,
therefore making bold with his Majefty's Houfe) and then they think they
can take a courfe both with the Parliament and City; which in truth they do
full handfomly.

191. For prefently they make them
refume the confideration of the Charge

O 3 againft

againſt the Lord *Willoughby*, and paſs it, and likewiſe againſt the reſt of thoſe Lords, and Sir *John Maynard* ; carry it up to the Houſe of Lords, and demand the recommitting of thoſe Lords, and putting them to their anſwer. Sir *Arthur Haſlerig*, the now worthy Governor of *Newcaſtle*, ſtaid in town from going to take poſſeſſion of his Command, only to do this feat ; ſo to make good what he before ſaid, when they could not upon a long debate, and the laying out of all their ſtrength and power, carry the Impeachment, that it was no matter, the Army ſhould impeach them all.

192. A little after the Lord *Grey* of *Groby* ſets on foot the motion concerning thoſe of the eleven Members who were beyond Sea, having had Paſſes to travel for ſix Months, and moſt of them written or ſent to the Speaker and other Gentlemen of the Houſe, to deſire the favor of a longer continuance, in regard it was winter, and ill croſſing the Seas ; but if it would not be granted, upon ſignification of their pleaſure, they would immediately return. They had likewiſe (upon occaſion of the Order of Summons) written

ten of the uncertain report they had heard
of such a thing long after it was done,
that if notice had been given them of it,
they had not fail'd to appear, and would
if they might be certify'd that the House
continu'd in the same resolution ; so confident were they of their innocency, tho
they knew the malice of their Enemies,
and their violence and force upon the Parliament : But proceedings since have made
it clear what Justice they should have
found.   For notwithstanding all this,
those Horse and Foot were so powerful
an argument against them, backing the
Remonstrance for the exclusive resolution, that it was carry'd to expel them
the House, and Impeachments order'd to
be brought in.   A parallel proceeding to
this was never known in Parliament,
where it has not been refus'd to any,
especially who were beyond Sea, or in
truth any where absent upon leave, to
give a further day upon non-appearance
the first; and in our Case there was a
great deal more reason, considering the
season of the year, the occasion of our
departure (then look'd upon as a merit)
our readiness to obey upon the first Summons.   All this writes but their Injustice
and our Oppression in the more Capital
Letters.   O 4   193.

193. I am now coming to the Ca-
taftrophe of this Tragedy, the laft and
moft horrid Act. The Parliament forc'd
to do that which is unnatural againft
the being of Parliament, the end for which
it is call'd, which has *rationem formæ* in all
moral things; that is, to declare they will
make no further addrefs or application to
the King, receive none from him, nor
fuffer it in others; which is, as if a Limb
fhould cut it felf off from the Body, and
thereby deprive it felf of life and nourifhment : For the communication between the King, and Parliament is that
which gives it being and life. It is call'd
by the King, *ad colloquium habendum &
tractatum cum proceribus Regni*, &c. They
are the words of the Writ which brings
them together. Now there is *Colloquium
& Tractatus* cut off, which was the firft
unhappy breach between his Majefty and
this Parliament, and which the Parliament found themfelves grieved at, that
he had withdrawn himfelf from them, fo
as they could not repair unto him for advice and counfel. And in all our Declarations and Meffages in the beginning, until
thefe people (who it feems had projected
from the firft what they have now acted)
got

got to the Helm, and ſteer'd us into this violent tempeſtuous Courſe, that we neither ſee our Pole, nor uſe our Compaſs ; we ſtill deſir'd, preſs'd, endeavour'd his Majeſty's return to his Parliament : But they ſay he ſhall not return, the Regal Power they have aſſum'd, they will keep it and exerciſe it. They will no longer be fellow Subjects with the reſt of the Kingdom, but Lords and Maſters. Thoſe whom they repreſent, and whoſe ſubſtitutes they are, they will put under their foot ; as if an Ambaſſadour ſhould renounce the Prince that ſent him, and ſay he will make his own Dignity real and original, which is but repreſentative and deriv'd, take away the ſubſtance and yet the ſhadow remain : certainly this is exceedingly againſt nature, and will turn all upſide down ; yet this diſorder muſt be made perpetual, put out of all poſſibility of recovery, like Death, from which there can be no returning. For admit the King would grant all that they have deſir'd or can deſire, give them all imaginable ſecurity for it, it is impoſſible it ſhould be made known, and ſo cannot be receiv'd, and by conſequence our Peace never be ſettled ; which is caſting the Kingdom into a mortal diſeaſe, putting it paſt cure, paſt hope. 194.

194. To shew by what Magick this Spirit is rais'd, you have his fellow Devil immediately call'd up by a Council of War; a Declaration comes from his Excellency and the general Council of the Army from *Windsor*, bearing date the 9*th* of *January*, presented to the House the 11*th* by Sir *Hardress Waller*, wherein they give their approbation of the Votes, say the Parliament in that Address to the King, with the four Bills, could go no lower without denying that which God, in the issue of War, had born such testimony unto : That they account that great business of a settlement to the Kingdom, and security to the publick interest thereof, by and with the King's concurrence, to be brought to so clear a trial, as that upon the King's denyal, they can see no further hopes of settlement and security that way ; therefore upon the consideration of that denyal, added to so many other such Votes as had been pass'd that no further application should be made to him, &c. They do freely and unanimously declare for themselves and the Army, that they are resolv'd firmly to adhere with and stand by the Parliament in the things so voted, and in

what

what shall be further necessary for the prosecution thereof, and for the settling and securing the Parliament and Kingdom without the King, and against the King, or any other that shall hereafter partake with him.

195. And in this I believe them, being (I am confident) the only truth has proceeded from them in all their Declarations or Proposals, with relation to his Majesty. I would remember them, if 'twere to any purpose, of some of their former professions, That it was against their principles to imprison the King, that no Peace could be lasting without him, and the like. But they can blow hot and cold, as the fellow in the Fable, to make all the Satyrs, and almost the Devil himself abhor them, as afraid to be outdone by them in his own art of lying and dissembling. Therefore I shall not trouble my self any more with blazoning their Goat Armour, which is nothing but false colours and base metals: Their Impostures, Contradictions, Falshoods, Hypocrisies, and damnable Delusions being beyond all Heraldry, not to be trick'd within the compass of any Scutcheon.

196. I will only add one Scene more
of this laft Act, reprefented in the Houfe
of Commons. I do not hear that the
Houfe of Peers have had any part in it.
But the Commons, like the Confiftory of
Rome, have fpent much time fince in hunting out the Premifes, to infer the Conclufion formerly agreed upon, a Declaration,
or rather rhetorical Invective, to perfwade
mens Affections, not convince their Judgments of thofe enormities in the King,
which fhould juftly merit, and fo juftifie the refolutions taken concerning him.
The particulars are fuch, as truly I cannot
name withont horror, *Auferat oblivio fi
poteft, fi non, filentium tegat :* I would
forget that ever fuch a thing was done
by the Parliament. I will only fay this
of that Faction (for I look upon it merely as their act and their Army's, who
have forc'd the Houfe to it, as they have
to all the reft fince the breaking out of
their Rebellion, the owning them, paying them, voting their continuance, expelling, committing, impeaching their
own Members, the Lord Mayor and Aldermen of the City of *London*, doing what
not for the encreafing their own fhame,
and fetting up their *Diana*, that Idol of
con-

confusion) That if they themselves believe that to be true which they there relate, they are excellent good Patriots, and notable Justices, to see and not see faults for their own advantage. For if the King would have agreed to such Conditions as they propos'd to him, and such a Settlement as had been in order to their Ends, to have continu'd an Omnipotency in them and ruin'd the rest of the Kingdom, these things had been all dispens'd with, sacrific'd to their greatness, and the advancement of their *Dagon*; then nothing but *Hosannah*'s in their mouths, no Peace could be lasting without due consideration of his Rights ; far was it from them to have a thought of imprisoning him, he had been their good King, and they his and our gracious Masters. But now that his Majesty had discover'd their aims, and would not contribute to them, he is an *Anathema*, guilty of such and so many crimes, as not to be found scarce in any one person ; and now these Men of *Belial* can say he shall not reign over us. For the things themselves, I doubt not but there are those who knowing the *Arcana Imperii*, will give satisfaction to the world by a faithful and clear manifestation of his Majesty's Actions and Counsels

fels relating to them. I who ftand below and at diftance, as I cannot have
the knowledg of fuch high things, fo
will not prefume to meddle with them,
only upon the general fay, that methinks
in reafon thofe things cannot be; for to
deftroy the Proteftants in *France*, whofe
prefervation muft needs be as a content-
ment to the Soul of a Proteftant King,
fo a ftrength and advantage to his Intereft, were ftrange State-policy. And
as for the Rebellion of *Ireland*, to cut
off fo great a Limb from himfelf, pluck
off one of the three Flowers of his Crown,
is, methinks, to be *Feio de fe.* To fpeak
nothing of that concerning King *James*,
an act fo monftrous as not to be fufpected in a Heathen, not to be found in hea-
thenifh *Rome*, much lefs in a Chriftian;
truly I cannot, as a rational Man, bring
my judgment to admit of a belief of
thofe things; and then certainly Charity
obliges to hope better, believe better of
any Man, much more of a King, and of
our own King, whom *Solomon* tells us
we are not to curfe, no, not in thought,
much lefs, which *Job* blames, tell him,
and tell the world he is wicked and un-
godly, leaft of all when there is not a
clear and undeniable proof. And even
their

their expreſſions in their Declaration are
not poſitive, as if the ſubjeƈt matter were
only *allegatum*, not at all *probatum*, and
rather ſet forth *ad captandum populum*, to
gain, if poſſible, an approbation of the
vulgar of what they had done, than that
they conceiv'd it would find credit with
rational and judicious Men, or that themſelves thought it to be a truth.   For the
other things, as Knighthood, Ship-money,
&c. any thing by which the Subjeƈt has
been oppreſs'd and his Purſe pick'd, they
of all Men ſhould not find fault, whoſe
little Finger has been heavier than the
Loins of Monarchy.   What was all that
in compariſon of free Quarter, Exciſe,
and even the 100000 *l.* a Month, which
they ſay they muſt have for the maintenance of the Army? thoſe were but
Flea-bitings to theſe.   At the worſt one
may ſay, we were then chaſtis'd with
Whips, but now with Scorpions.

197. And ſo I hope I have made good
what I undertook in the beginning, having made it appear, that *England* is
become, by the aƈtings of theſe Men,
that Monſter whoſe ſhape is perverted,
the head ſtanding where the feet, and
the feet where the head ſhould be, mean

Men

Men mounted aloft, and all that is or
should be great, Lacqueying it after
them: The authority of the Magiftrate
fuppress'd, and the will of particular
perfons made the Law of the Kingdom,
Juftice obftructed, and Violence in the
room of it; King and Parliament trodden
under foot, and an Army infulting over
the Perfons and Eftates of the Subject;
fo as we may take up the Pfalmift's
Complaint, That the very Foundations
are deftroy'd, and what then can the
Righteous do?

198. I will conclude all with this
fhort Epiphonema: If fuch a complica-
ted Treafon as this, which they have
defign'd and carry'd on all along, confifting of fo many feveral parts, by betraying all the Trufts Men can be capa-
ble of, as Subjects to their King, Servants
to their Mafters, an Army to them that
rais'd and paid them, Englifh Men to their
Country, and which is more, Chriftians
to their God, bound up yet in a more
particular obligation by Covenant, Vows,
and Proteftations; all thefe Relations
thrown afide, nothing of Duty, Confcience, or Morality to ftand in the way,
that could either be remov'd or overcome,

come; eluded or broken through. If, I say, a Treafon rais'd up to this height, by fo many feveral fteps of Hypocrifie, Treachery, Perfidioufnefs, Injuftice, Violence, and Cruelty, can be made good, and the Actors profper, blefling themfelves in their fuccefs, facrificing to their Nets and Gins, by which they have fnar'd and deftroy'd all their oppofers : And on the other fide, if no blefling muft be on the good endeavours of thofe who only had propos'd to themfelves *Bonum publicum,* had nothing in particular in their Eye, fought nothing for themfelves, but to find their fafety compris'd and contain'd in the happinefs and welfare of the King, Parliament, and Kingdom ; like the honeft Paffengers that feek their prefervation in faving the Ship they fail in (as I can fpeak it for a truth, take the God of Heaven for Witnefs, and defie all the Men on Earth to difprove it) that I for my part (and I hope the fame of thofe other perfons of Honour, Members of both Houfes, with whom I have cooperated, and now partake in their fufferings) never had other end : Let the Earl of *Manchefter* fpeak, who has been prefent at and privy to all our Confultations, and is now join'd and engag'd with the Army, and thofe

P other

other Men who carry on this pernicious
defign, where, befides the univerfal de-
folation of the whole Kingdom, there is
a particularity againft me for my ruin
and deftruction, and therefore I doubt
not but he will fay all he knows: Let
Mr. *Reynolds* of the Houfe of Commons,
who went a long time and a great way
with us, but is fince fallen off and become
throughly theirs; the fame I fay of Colonel *Harvy*, who was long enough in
our Ears, and in our Bofoms, to bottom
all our thoughts, know all our defires.
If thefe or any other, even that malicious and treacherous Lord *Savil*, can fay,
that at any time, upon any occafion, I
propos'd any thing that look'd towards
a felf End, the driving of any particular
Intereft, fetting up of any Party, but
merely to prevent thefe fearful Precipi-
ces into which the Kingdom is fallen,
by the art and practices of thefe Enemies of Peace, and to attain fuch a fettlement, as all honeft moderate Men
might have found in it both fecurity and
fatisfaction: If they can, let them fpeak;
and if they prove one tittle, I will put
my Mouth in the duft, I will bear my
punifhment, and expect mercy neither
from God nor Man; nay, even in relation to the Army, and thofe perfons who
have

have a long time fought my ruin, if all
I defir'd and aim'd at in disbanding that
fchifmatical factious Soldiery, in carrying
on the bufinefs of the Houfe in oppofition to that Party, and even in this laft
great Treafon of levying War againft
King, Parliament, and Kingdom (as they
ftile it) which was only to do my beft
endeavour to defend them and my felf
from a rebellious Army that was marching up for all our deftructions, contrary
to the Orders of both Houfes, againft
whom it firft rebell'd inftead of an obedient disbanding; then cudgel'd them to
own it for their Army, forc'd the City
into a trouble, and fhew of oppofition to
what it had made the Parliament do;
then took that occafion to march both
againft it and the Parliament. If notwithftanding all this, in what I did, I
had any thought of perfonal revenge, or
to do the leaft hurt to any particular
perfon in cafe we had prevail'd, but only to return into the way whence we
were put out, of a free quiet Parliamentary
proceeding, to accomplifh the great work
of fettling the Peace both of Church and
State, let me perifh; and God, who is
the fearcher of hearts, knows I now
fpeak nothing but truth.

199. Well then, I fay, if all our endeavours muft, like an untimely birth,
come to nothing, our hope be cut off,
our perfons deftroy'd, our integrity, innocency, fidelity queftion'd and decry'd,
our good names traduc'd, torn in funder,
our memories made to ftink to all pofterity, by the falfe calumnies of our
malicious Enemies, and their power in
fuppreffing truth, and which is worft
(for all this is but particular) the general, the publick, the Common wealth,
once in fo fair a way of recovery, at the
eve of a happy day, to be rid of Armies,
enjoy a Peace, hear no more of the Inftruments of War, but fee a bleffed com-
pofure of all unhappy differences, reap
the fruits of Juftice and Mercy; and upon a fudden to find all this but as the
hungry man's Dream, who is the more
empty when he awakes, fo inftead of
this folid happinefs to embrace a Cloud,
have nothing but the empty promifes of
a falfe deceitful Army, and be caft back
into a greater gulf of mifery and confufion than all the enemies in the World
could have brought it into, and the latter end to be far worfe than the beginning:

200. If this be our Portion, were I a Heathen, I should say with *Brutus* when he meant to kill himself, seeing the assertors of publick Liberty overcome and ruin'd, and the Invaders prevail and conquer, *O misera virtus! eras igitur fabula, seu verba; ego te ut rem colebam & exercebam, tu autem fortuna serviebas.* But being a Christian, I am taught another Lesson, to know that nothing comes by chance. God, who dos all things in number, weight, and measure, orders and disposes all as may most make for his own Honour, and the good of his Church and Children, to which even the wickedness of the wicked, and these Disorders will conduce, tho the wit of Man cannot fathom it: therefore I will lay my Hand upon my Mouth, and not once whisper, because the Lord has done it, only take up St. *Paul's* admiration, and with it end, crying out, *O Altitudo! O the Depth of the Riches both of the Wisdom and Knowledg of God! How unsearchable are his Judgments, and his Ways past finding out!*

FINIS.

AN

Alphabetical Table.

A.

The TABLE.

P 4

on

The TABLE.

The TABLE.

The TABLE.

D.

D.

E.

F.

The TABLE.

H.

H.

I.

Joyce,

The TABLE.

The TABLE.

M.

Q.   Fot.

The TABLE.

O.

O.

P.

point

The TABLE.

R.

The TABLE.

The TABLE.

The TABLE.

FINIS.

LEX *Parliamentaria;* or, a Treatise of the Law and Custom of the Parliaments of *England*, by *G. P.* Esq; with an Appendix of a Case in Parliament between Sir *Francis Goodwin* and Sir *John Fortescue*, for the Knights Place for the County of *Bucks.* 1 *Jac.* 1.

Reflections upon what the World commonly calls *good Luck* and *ill Luck*, with regard to Lotteries, and of the good use which may be made of them. Written in French by Monsieur *Le Clerc*, and done into English.

Printed for *Tim. Goodwin.*

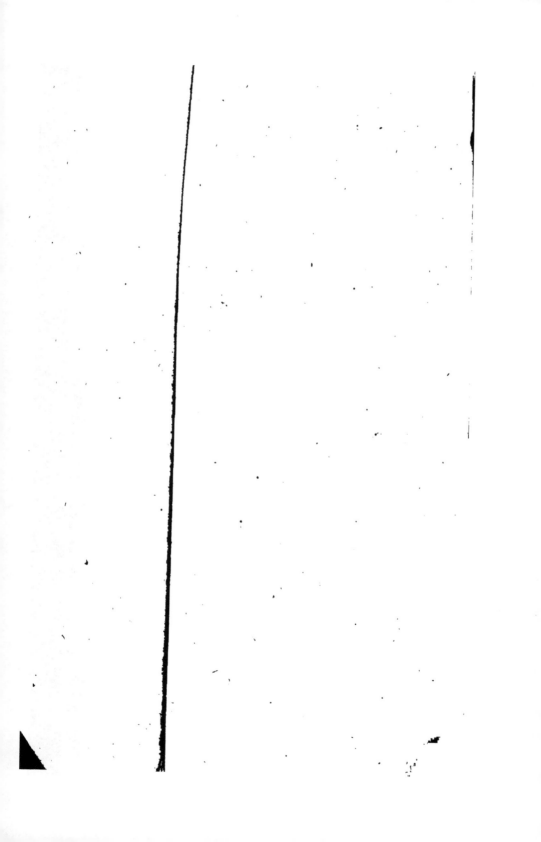

Lightning Source UK Ltd.
Milton Keynes UK
UKHW021239181119
353758UK00010B/2628/P